Young
Sober
&Free

"An excellent guide! . . . Give it to the millions of parents, counselors, and teens who need it."

—Toby Rice Drews, author of the *Getting Them Sober* books

"In reading *Young, Sober & Free,* I am overwhelmed by the intuitive brilliance of our youth as they rebelliously toss aside the shackles of addiction. Marshall has successfully captured this sense of 'natural knowing' and wisdom beyond their years. No matter the age, if someone in your life is struggling with addictions, share with them this streetwise mosaic of recovery."

—Dan McFadden, author of *Cheechako*

"*Young, Sober & Free* is highly recommended reading for our youthful clients and their families."

—Henry F. Gokee, M.A., C.D.P., N.C.A.C. II,
director of Colonial Clinic

Young Sober &Free

Experience, Strength, and Hope for Young Adults

SECOND EDITION

WRITTEN AND COMPILED BY

SHELLY MARSHALL

■ HAZELDEN®

Hazelden
Center City, Minnesota 55012-0176

1-800-328-0094
1-651-213-4590 (Fax)
www.hazelden.org

Library of Congress Cataloging-in-Publication Data
    Marshall, Shelly.
      Young, sober & free: experience, strength, and hope for young adults /
    Shelly Marshall.— 2nd ed.
        p. cm.
      Previously published: San Francisco: Harper/Hazelden, 1987, c1978.
      ISBN 1-56838-986-8 (paperback)
      1. Alcoholism—Case studies. 2. Narcotic habit—Case studies. 3. Youth—
    Alcohol use. 4. Youth—Drug use. I. Title: Young, sober, and free. II. Title.

    RC565.M319 2003
    362.292'0835—dc21

                                                              2002038897

07 06 05 04 03   6 5 4 3 2 1

Editor's note
All of the stories in this book are based on actual experiences. Many of the names and details have been changed to protect the privacy of the people involved. In some cases composites have been created.

    The Twelve Steps of AA are reprinted and adapted with permission of Alcoholics Anonymous World Services, Inc. (AAWS). Permission to reprint and adapt the Twelve Steps does not mean that AAWS has reviewed or approved the contents of this publication or that AAWS necessarily agrees with the views expressed herein. AA is a program of recovery from alcoholism *only*; use of the Twelve Steps in connection with programs and activities which are patterned after AA, but which address other problems, or in any other non-AA context, does not imply otherwise.

Cover design by David Spohn
Interior design by David Spohn
Typesetting by Stanton Publication Services, Inc.

Dedication

We (Shelly Marshall and the numerous young contributors to *Young, Sober & Free*) want to express our gratitude to Craig Fraiser for mentioning our book in his book. Craig courageously told his story of adolescent addiction and recovery in *Burnt: A Teenage Addict's Road to Recovery* and referred to *Young, Sober & Free* as having helped form the foundation for his understanding of addiction and recovery:

> *Young, Sober & Free* taught me some new things about addiction. As I sat there in my hospital room with time to absorb the information in the book, it dawned on me that maybe I didn't know as much about drugs as I thought I did. (*Burnt: A Teenage Addict's Road to Recovery*, New American Library, 1990, p. 201)

We are humbled and honored that our book has launched the recovery of countless young addicts and alcoholics like Craig. It is to all of us in the YES crowd (Youth Enjoying Sobriety), and those we wait for, that these pages are dedicated.

Contents

Preface

Millions of men and women once stricken with the demoralizing disease of dependency to various mind-affecting/mood-altering drugs, including alcohol, now glowingly speak in almost every tongue of their personal miracle of recovery. They speak not only from every tongue, but from every age group, including preadolescents, adolescents, and young adults. Indeed, it is from the YES crowd (Youth Enjoying Sobriety) that *Young, Sober & Free* has come into being. Although the primary author and compiler of this book is Shelly Marshall, neither the first edition nor this revision would have been feasible without the combined efforts of young people's recovery groups, students from sober high schools, adolescents in treatment, and incarcerated youth. The ideas, recovery stories, and commitment come from the camaraderie of "Youth Enjoying Sobriety" and thus the "we" referred to in these pages includes these contributors.

Each new generation launches fresh ideas into our society, infuses new energy into old customs, and eventually latches on to the values that have become the foundation of our great country. This is as true for our programs of recovery as it is for society in general. This revision reflects the fresh ideas and the contemporary customs of today's youth while the foundation of the recovery text remains embedded in the Twelve Step traditions and Step principles. The most notable changes in this revision of *Young, Sober & Free* are found in the terminology surrounding drugs, addiction, and recovery. Next, the ongoing discoveries and contributions of science regarding addiction and brain chemistry are included. Our understanding of the disease of addiction is so much clearer today than when this book first came out. As a result, the drug classifications and discussion of our disease have been duly updated. Five new stories have been added. One of these stories is from a young addict's mother who reaches out to help other parents suffering the same anguish. Although only ten stories are listed in the table of contents of this revised edition (there were fourteen in the first edition), the old classics *are not gone*. Rather, each of these stories is presented in quotes and examples throughout the text.

The most important differences between the two editions are found in chapter 7, which is addressed to parents. When the first edition came out, I, Shelly, was one of the young people in recovery. Many years later, I am one of the parents too! When my seventeen-year-old daughter entered treatment, my "take" on parents and addicted youth made a 180-degree turn. A blessing in disguise, this turn of events allowed me to rewrite the parent's perspective from a truly knowledgeable base. For parents who turn to this chapter looking for help, you might have to give up control, *but never give up hope*. After a long and very painful journey, my girl is not only clean and sober, but happily married and raising three of the most beautiful children on earth!

Although many paths lead to recovery, those of us who put this book together have found our core recovery through the various Twelve Step fellowships modeled after Alcoholics Anonymous. These Twelve Step fellowships include

> Alcoholics Anonymous (AA)
> Chemically Dependent Anonymous (CDA)
> Cocaine Anonymous (CA)
> Marijuana Anonymous (MA)
> Narcotics Anonymous (NA)
> Pills Anonymous (PA)

In the words we have set down in this book, we only repeat what has been given us by the fellowships referenced above. It isn't our intention to begin a new program or fellowship. Our message is tailored specifically for young people (and their parents) and meant to supplement the existing books and literature about recovery. We remember always that we are members of AA, NA, CDA, and other related fellowships and that any controversies are to be settled within our home groups through group conscience.

We have written this book to reach out to our young fellow sufferers in the hope that they may accept help sooner rather than later, avoiding years of suffering, heartache, and premature death. You see, we know that all addicts stop using eventually; we just want them to be alive when that happens.

We have found a way that works and wish to share it with you. If you find you can use our model of recovery, we heartily welcome you and hope you experience our joy in living *Young, Sober & Free.*

Acknowledgments

We would like to acknowledge the many young people, professionals, parents, and members of the Twelve Step programs who so generously supported the compilation of this book. It isn't possible to list all of those who contributed either directly or indirectly to these pages. However, of special note for this second edition are the contributions from the more recently developed sober high schools and especially the support of the National Association of Recovery Schools, particularly Judy Ide, the principal of Community High School, a program of Creative Recovery Communities, Inc.

CHAPTER 1

Never Too Young

*"It's a good thing I'm not too young to be an alcoholic.
I probably wouldn't live long enough to become old enough."*
—Teddy

Not too many years ago, a lot of people thought that alcoholics were men (no one wanted to believe that women could be drunks) who had lost their jobs, their families, and even a decent place to live. Alcoholics and addicts, they thought, were a subpopulation of the homeless living in shelters, under bridges, and in boxes. They were gutter people. Whole communities denied that a person as young as fifteen or sixteen could be a *real* alcoholic, and community leaders doubted that "properly raised" adolescents injected narcotics, snorted coke, or dealt drugs. Today we know better.

As young addicts, we don't question that people under twenty-five can experience alcoholism and other brutal drug addictions, but parents and professionals often think we're too young to be in the same predicament as the gutter people. Although they understand that substance *abuse* is rampant among young people, they don't realize that chemical dependency *is a disease.* Some of us really, truly, honestly suffer from a clinical disease. It's not "abuse," a "phase," or youthful rebellion.

Parents, professionals, and community leaders *do know* that something to do with drugs has gone wrong, but they don't know why. Parents want to blame the public schools and ill-begotten friends; professionals often try to blame bad parenting and poor communication skills; aspects of the legal system may emphasize socioeconomic factors; while some religious folks might think we're lacking in morality. These well-meaning individuals tell us we're "too nice, too smart, or too young" to be *real* addicts and alcoholics. And, of course, until we young addicts embrace recovery, we're only too willing to agree. We also agree that our drug use and abuse isn't our fault. Let's blame our out-of-control behavior on the schools, our friends, the uncertain state of the world, our parents, and any other handy pretext *but* the fact that we can't stop using!

We Didn't Use Drugs and Alcohol—They Used Us

This book is for you if

- you're seriously questioning your own substance use and abuse
- your alibis have fallen apart
- you're asking yourself, "Am I or am I not an alcoholic and/or addict?"

We have compiled this book to share what we've learned about addiction and recovery. We are young people from all over the country who have found a solution to the devastating destruction of obsessively using and abusing all manner of mind-affecting chemicals. Whether you're a pothead, huffer head, E-head, or dead head, whether you downed shots or shot downers, if you're sick and tired of the self-loathing, trouble dogging you, parents pleading with you, and courts punishing you, then this book is our gift to you.

We start with our attitude. Our definition and understanding of the disease of addiction greatly affect our attitudes and chances of recovery. Consider the following:

- Even if I have to stop drinking, I can still smoke marijuana because it's nonaddictive.
- I can stop using for a few years, get my head together, and then be able to have a couple drinks now and again.
- Alcoholism isn't the same as taking club drugs or using steroids.
- I'm too young; after all, my parents have been drinking for years.

If you believe these statements, then you don't yet understand the complex nature of our illness. You are not alone. Many people don't understand addiction, and it was only through hard knocks, reading recovery literature, and listening to those who went before us that we reached a basic understanding of chemical dependency. Many will not agree with us. This is all right; they are entitled to their opinion. However, it is *our* lives and freedom that are endangered. If you find that you don't really use drugs and alcohol but that *they use you,* then you'll want to explore this disease with us.

What Is Addiction?

What we see in young people who are hooked on one or more mind-affecting chemical is a physical compulsion, a mental obsession, and a serious lack of a spiritual base, sometimes called "self-centeredness." People who are addicted are preoccupied with their drug of choice, never wanting to go anyplace where they don't have access to their drug. For example, think of the father who won't go to a restaurant that doesn't serve beer or the high school student who quit the swim team because she or he couldn't easily sneak cocaine during matches and practice.

An old-fashioned concept in psychology claimed there was such a thing as an "addictive personality," but in recent years that theory has pretty much disappeared. Some people argue that the drug itself has the power to entrap and hook the addict, yet many people use highly addictive drugs and never succumb to addiction. Patients recovering from surgery are often given morphine for pain. They build up a tolerance and even have withdrawal symptoms when taken off the painkiller, but after discharge they don't roam the streets, committing burglaries in search of the drug. They simply go back to their normal lives. Just as we would not say that "addictive dice" entrap compulsive gamblers, it isn't the drugs alone that get us but a combination of components. Chemical dependency doesn't seem to be about a particular substance or a personality type but about the *relationship* they form on a physical, mental, and spiritual plane with the addicted.

Physical Compulsion: One Is Too Much and a Thousand Never Enough

First, let's discuss the physical compulsion. This compulsion can perhaps best be described as the body craving drugs, possibly even to its own destruction. When you have that craving, your brain may or may not give its okay. You know that you shouldn't have another fix, pill, drink, tok, or snort, yet you *want* it and *want it bad*. You take the first drink; you take the tok; you snort the line, and *it isn't enough*. You want another, then another. This is how we came to know that one is too much and a thousand never enough. Once you take that one, you're probably not done until something stops you—like Mom or Dad or the law—or you pass out or run out of dope, money, or friends. Lori describes her compulsion this way:

> I never really thought too much about not having control over my drinking, but time after time I found myself drunk when I didn't want to be. Even then, I thought I was cool, but I started having blackouts and I'd make the biggest fool of myself, so I was told. I started cutting classes to drink and finally just stopped going to school. I wasn't off with my friends having a good time. I wasn't with a boyfriend. I was home by myself, drinking and watching TV, drinking until I passed out or until I cried myself to sleep. Booze wasn't fun anymore. It ruined every form of relationship with guys, and most of my friends even stopped calling. A drunk girl wasn't a very pretty sight, especially when it was me.

A Drug Is a Drug Is a Drug

Drugs of abuse fall into five distinct categories:

Depressants: alcohol, barbiturates, benzodiazepines, methaqualone, narcotics
Commonly called barbs, heroin, junk, ludes, oxy, Special K
Ergogenic drugs: anabolic steroids
Commonly called muscle juice, roids, steroids

Hallucinogenics: LSD, marijuana, MDMA (3,4-methylene-
dioxymethamphetamine), mushrooms, peyote, phencyclidine
Commonly called acid, buttons, Ecstasy, hash, weed, PCP, shrooms,
THC, X
Inhalants: gasoline, household chemicals, industrial solvents,
nitrites
Commonly called huffing agents, head cleaners, poppers, whippets
Stimulants: amphetamines, cocaine, methamphetamines
Commonly called coke, crack, crank, crystal meth, glass, powder,
white

These drugs are also known by slang words that often change. We
listed only the expressions that have fallen into everyday language.

It doesn't matter whether we abused "designer drugs" (drugs that
are chemically altered in order to escape legal control), OTCs (over-the-
counter drugs), prescriptions, legal drugs, or illegal drugs. A drug is a
drug is a drug. Or if you want to get more technical: a mind-affecting
chemical is a mind-affecting chemical is a . . . well, you get the point.

We know that most depressants and stimulants are highly addictive. Experts disagree, however, about whether the other categories of
drugs are addictive. Some research has shown that steroids may be addictive. We won't enter into the controversy over the addictive or nonaddictive properties of hallucinogenics and inhalants. However, we are
reminded of the guy who, when asked if pot was addicting, replied, "It
can't be. I've smoked it every day for five years!"

It is known that once a person is addicted to any drug in a particular class, he or she has built up a tolerance for any drug in that same
class. Tolerance—needing more and more to get the same high—is the
first stage of dependency. In later stages of dependency, tolerance can
reverse so one needs less to get high, sometimes putting an addict or alcoholic in danger of overdosing while *decreasing* their use. However, in
earlier stages, if you chippy a little heroin and get a nice high, your
body gets accustomed to it and it takes a little more each time you use
to get high again. This means that if you go to a hospital in severe pain,

it's going to take more morphine to relieve the pain than it would for the average person who hasn't built up a tolerance. If you're dependent on tranquilizers and have developed a tolerance for them and then later drink, you'll need more alcohol to get high, whether you drink often or not. Theoretically, a person might show classic signs of alcoholism without having a drinking history.

Switching from One Drug to Another Is Like Switching Seats on the *Titanic*

"Well, okay," a person says, "I agree that I'm addicted to heroin, and I believe that other depressants like alcohol will trigger my compulsion, but there's no reason why I can't smoke pot or snort a little coke." Ah, yes. This is a thought many of us have entertained, sometimes until we had no thoughts left at all. Remember, chemical dependency isn't about a particular substance or a personality type but about the *relationship* they form on a physical, mental, and spiritual plane. This "relationship" between us and chemicals means that if we can't get our drug of choice, then probably anything will do. We're called garbage heads.

Suzi, thirteen, who'd been drinking in bars with the "big people" for years, remembers starting drugs there:

> I used LSD, speed, glue, paint remover, and downers. It didn't take long before I was shooting barbs, speed, and heroin, although shooting was something I said I would never do. It seemed that it just happened one night when I was already loaded and the people I was with told me how really great and fast shooting was. I thought that it wouldn't hurt to try. I did and I liked it. And things got worse.

So, is Suzi an alcoholic, speed freak, huffer head, or heroin addict? *She is chemically dependent.* Even experts in addictionology and the mental health fields do not entirely agree about what constitutes chemical dependency. However, it's clearly a disease. Most professionals agree, for instance, that addiction is a neurobiological disorder, but they aren't sure what *causes* the disorder. Most experts agree that there's often a genetic component and that chronic use may alter the brain, predisposing one to addiction. Some even think that chronic stressors and repeated behaviors may affect the brain's susceptibility to addiction. Traditionally, the definition for addiction included

1. the craving for a high (euphoria)
2. tolerance (needing more and more to get high)
3. withdrawal (painful and flu-like symptoms upon stopping use)

The picture isn't so clear though when you throw in steroids (which don't seem to produce much euphoria) and hallucinogenics and inhalants (which don't seem to produce the usual withdrawal symptoms). What is very clear and true of all addictions is this: *uncontrolled use despite negative consequences.*

Examine Your Head
Using despite negative consequences begs the question of the mental aspect. When you keep using even when you promise you won't, even though you get into trouble, even when you risk losing your girlfriend or boyfriend or going to jail, then you have to examine your head. What's going on? Well, we're high chasers. We would rather feel happy than sad, euphoric than down. We want to feel smooth and easy. *We want to roll.* We use all kinds of excuses for using when cornered, like blaming our parents or the "system" for being too restrictive and controlling. If they aren't oppressive, then we blame them for neglecting us and not disciplining us. They didn't pay enough attention to us or they pushed too hard; they didn't give us enough or they gave us too much; they didn't talk with us or they lectured us—whatever fits will do. The truth is that we wanted what we wanted when we wanted it, and that was to get high and feel happy. So what's so bad about wanting to feel happy?

Nothing. Wanting that dizzy-light-somewhere-else feeling is not bad. So many people have that desire that it's safe to call it completely natural. Even kids have it. Observe children at the playground; the thrill of a merry-go-round is actually that dizzy-light-somewhere-else feeling. How about kids holding their breath and trying to faint or spinning in circles until they lose their balance? What about the most popular rides at an amusement park?

The feelings we seek are not sick or unnatural. However, our wires got tangled up somewhere along the neural pathway, because in our use, we keep seeking the high even when the good feelings have disappeared, when our use is obviously self-destructive, when we can't remember the trip, and when people don't like us anymore. We con ourselves: "This time it'll be different; I got into trouble because of my stupid friends (parents, police, circumstances, the dog—whatever). I'll smoke weed instead of drinking beer; I'll pop pills instead of shooting up; I'll drink wine instead of snorting a line." This is the point at which we should recognize our insanity; yet we seldom do. We're like John, who contributed to *Young, Sober & Free* from prison:

> The only drug I have never taken is heroin because of my fear of getting hooked. I never considered myself hooked on anything except cigarettes. Just because I was always taking some drug, and never in moderation, didn't mean I was hooked. It is a shame how badly we deceive ourselves. Everything I did, wherever I went, booze and drugs were included. They were the power of my life. I got into a "contest" with my girl who had a script for Phenobarbital. We took five tabs apiece and one every five minutes. Nine tabs and three days later, I crawled out of bed. She was in the hospital. Next day I was back to shooting speed and smoking pot with a bottle close by. A month later I downed a four-way tab of acid and had to bring myself down on Thorazine. I could run stories like these all day. I was always taking more than enough and it was never enough for me.

The Spiritual Side to This Disease Is Called "Self-Centeredness"

While using, our mental obsession about our drug use may not seem all that selfish. We're just having a good time, we say. And this brings us to the third component in our disease, the spiritual malady. We are unquestionably conscious of *our* needs, *our* desires, *our* problems, *our* abilities—and maybe even *our* faults. In short, we're *self-centered* people. Self-centered is not spiritual. Any working connection with a loving, creative Higher Power or being of service to our fellow man is practically nonexistent in our using lives. Our reliance is on chemicals, not on God. Our energy is directed toward a drug, not our family and friends.

Eventually we find ourselves in this sad state. We have a compulsion to drink and use, even when we don't want to. Normal activities and our loved ones take a back seat to our drug of choice. We become loners in a sea of self, only superficially tending to others to fulfill our needs. From such a superficial and shallow world, we hit bottom.

It is from this despair that we begin to seek help. Phil, who was introduced to the program when his dad stopped drinking, described his awakening like this:

> After trying to drink rather than do drugs, I realized that I was powerless over all drugs and that my life was truly unmanageable. I was at a point where I was willing to do *anything* in this world to get better—to stop living the way I hated so much, but I was trapped. I saw that if I was to keep from killing myself, I needed help. I couldn't do it alone. Then a truly amazing thing happened to me. Once I admitted that I was an alcoholic, things began to change. It was as if all other truths were blocked until I faced this truth. Once I was honest about my alcoholism, a world of things unseen about myself opened up and I began to change.

Here are the Steps that worked for us. Knowing what we now know about our disease, we begin Step One:

Step 1: We admitted we were powerless over mood-changing and mind-altering chemicals and that our lives had become unmanageable.*

"But I'm *not* powerless," is the cry of most beginners. Jason described it this way:

> I had a hard time accepting the idea that I was an alcoholic because when I would drink, I might not lose control that particular time. But it would start a process in me that I couldn't stop. To be an alcoholic I thought I had to drink a beer and five days later find myself with no money in a cheap hotel in another state. I saw that as powerlessness. Then I realized that I had absolutely no power in stopping my downward slide into trouble; my gradual intake of alcohol became greater, and my ill feelings toward myself and others grew. I didn't feel this way because I wanted to. I tried not to, but I simply couldn't control it and that showed me powerlessness.

The terms *alcoholic, chemically dependent,* and *addict,* mean something different to each person, so it's important to accept the general concept of powerlessness before pinning a label on yourself that you may not fully believe or understand. On the whole, we don't fret about labels like pothead, pill head, huffer head, druggy, junkie, or drunk. Our drug of choice isn't very important. In Step One we simply admit our powerlessness over intoxicants. Either we are or we aren't; there is no middle ground. Either our way with chemicals worked or it didn't. If it didn't, then we must admit that our lives had become unmanageable.

---

* The Twelve Steps of Chemically Dependent Anonymous are listed individually as they are discussed in the text. For a complete list of the Twelve Steps from Alcoholics Anonymous, Narcotics Anonymous, and Chemically Dependent Anonymous, see the appendix.

No, Your Honor, My Life Is Not Unmanageable!
Being young, it's more difficult to see unmanageability as anything significant. After all, don't we have the rest of our lives to get a grip on it? So we begin comparing ourselves to others who are worse off and do incredibly more stupid or wicked things. This minimizes our perception of "unmanageability" and becomes a barrier to true acceptance of our condition. Mary Beth explains it this way:

> I had a certain definition in my mind of an addict. First it was a person who acted like a different person while stoned—that hadn't happened to me yet. When it did, an addict became someone who was getting into car wrecks. That hadn't happened to me yet; then it did. It went on. An addict was someone who was late and delinquent in school, then a dropout, then someone who couldn't remember the night before, etc. As I hit each level, my definition of an addict kept going down to the next level.

Identify, Don't Compare
Anytime we compare ourselves to others in deciding whether or not we have a problem, we'll always find those worse off than we are. We can always use comparisons to our advantage so that we look good. The only valid comparison is that of ourselves to ourselves over a period of time. Am I better today than I was yesterday? Am I better this month compared with last month or last year?

There are a few other questions we can ask ourselves in determining our own addiction:

• Do mind-affecting, mood-altering chemicals affect the way I feel about myself, my friends, the people around me?
• Do I seem to be in a downward spiral?

The point is not, "Am I an alcoholic?" but, "Can I drink and take dope and be peaceful with my life as a whole?" Chemical dependency is a progressive disease. It gets worse, never better, and for people chanting the "not yets," it's only a question of time.

The Party's Not Over

Contrary to what you might delude yourself with, waiting to take Step One doesn't add years to the fun of partying and getting high. It adds years to the disaster and heartache, *if* you live through those years, that is. Many of our peers died in the car wreck when we survived, died in the drive-by shooting that missed us, died from the overdose that a pump in our stomach saved us from, or fried their brains on PCP on one more trip than we took.

Remember, no one goes to jail, drops out of school, or gets pregnant from eating peanut butter. If mind-affecting, mood-altering chemicals create problems in your life, then you have a drug problem. The only constant definition for addiction is simple: *uncontrolled use despite negative consequences.*

And that is what we call "unmanageable."

CINDY'S STORY

Cindy is seventeen years old and has three years' sobriety.

At fourteen, I was lucky. I found help. I always pictured an alcoholic as a male, approximately seventy years old, who slept in gutters and on park benches and carried a cheap bottle of whiskey around in a brown paper sack. Today, when I think of someone who fits that description, I have to laugh. Boy, was I wrong!

Chugalugging at Three

I started drinking when I was about three years old. Oh, not real drinking, but that's when I got my start. My dad used to let me have sips of his beer. I would lift the bottle up, put it to my lips, open my throat, and let it pour. I was chugalugging at three! I would then hand the half-empty bottle back to my dad, walk through the door, and promptly fall flat on my face. I was a real adult. In these early moments of drinking, I discovered something that urged me on in my drinking career: When I drank, I felt that I fit right in with the adults and I was comfortable. I also found that everyone liked me and that I received a lot of attention.

By the time I was five, I was allowed to drink a whole bottle or two, if I could hold that much beer, and I began to learn to plan, eventually planning how I would manage to sneak an extra bottle or how to smuggle some beer into my lunch Thermos to take to school.

From then on much of my life is a blank. I remember I had a mean first-grade teacher, a nice second-grade teacher, and I was bombed in third grade. By fifth grade I would get the shakes when I couldn't find booze. I lived in a fantasy world with make-believe parents in a make-believe place. In sixth grade I finally found friends (and enemies). I found a few people who drank and we quickly became buddies. I also recall getting in fights with kids and teachers because I was loud, rude, and obnoxious. At those times, I always got sent out to sit on the steps, and I loved it because all of the "cool" people would be on the steps and I wanted to be one of the cool ones.

My Book Locker Became a Liquor Cabinet

Over the next two years, my drinking changed, and so did my life. I discovered a new, large group of friends and a new, large world of drugs. Many things happened during this time. My parents were separated; I was suspended from school and busted for shoplifting; I delved heavily into drugs, started pushing drugs, and totally withdrew. In school I didn't have a book locker; I had a liquor cabinet. I joined a gang of kids who practically ran the school, and there were some pretty large guys who would protect me from harm. All of this was really cool. In this situation, I tried many different drugs and became addicted to many. Reality began to fade in and out for me.

I seemed to form two separate personalities. At times I would wish someone would put me away. I thought I was crazy and many times I dreamed of death. Depression became so heavy that I wanted to take my life, but I became too apathetic to take any action on it. I couldn't sleep without help, and help came in taking pills in outrageous amounts to put me on my way.

One day, just to get through the school day, I accidentally took an overdose of pills. I never knew what those pills were, but I took too many. Along came strange visions, and in panic I began pulling out my hair. By the end of the day I had bald spots on my head and I was so weak that I had to be carried home. By this time I had had quite a few experiences with blackouts. People were always telling me what a good time I had at a party that I didn't even know I had been at. It frightened me when I came to in places I had never been before. I began to expect that something might be wrong with me, but I was still far from admitting it.

Happiness through Osmosis

At last, a friend conned me into going to the Palmer Drug Abuse Program—a Twelve Step program based mostly in Texas. When I first went, I found the people had something I wanted, so I hung around and really thought I could get their happiness through osmosis. I tried to stay straight and it worked for a while.

Then, suddenly, it all changed. One day my parents told my brother and me that we were moving to Denver. It seemed like not even a week went by before we were packed and on the road. I hated Denver and I hated the people there, but in an effort to show my friends back home in Houston how well I was doing, I tried to stay straight. It seemed to me that I could turn over a new leaf and finally be the person I always wanted to be.

But the leaf was not formed. Not more than a month went by in Denver before I was high again. Where had the willpower to turn down any offers gone? Within a week, there staggered the drunk kid again. It wasn't long before I eliminated school because I no longer cared about anything, including myself.

Out of desperation, I called AA and asked about where I should go. Not more than five minutes later, a lady named Pat called me back. She picked me up that night and took me to an AA meeting. It seemed to me that several people in the meeting resented my being there because I was so young, and one man even confronted me, saying he had spilled more than I ever drank. I was stunned. But Pat told me not to let him bother me. Soon afterward I learned to reply, "If you drank all you say you spilled, you would have gotten here as soon as I did too" or "What do you think I've been on, a picnic?"

A Teenage AA Group

A lot of good came out of that first night. Pat and I talked on the way home and we decided to start a teenage AA group. I relied on Pat for my sobriety for a while. But I knew this could not last. Finally we got a place in a church to use for our meetings, and for months we stared at each other, and we talked, and we talked. Finally one night someone else showed up and from then on the group quickly grew. In fact, recently it has been crowded.

I grew right along with the group. I began working my Steps more rigorously and have had many beautiful Twelfth Step calls. I found that the longer I was around AA, the more acceptance I received from older people. I love young people's groups, but I have found that I need the regular meetings to make my program complete.

The Thorns in My Rose Garden
Over the few years that I've been sober, I have learned about the thorns in my rose garden. One of the sharpest thorns was my social life. I wanted to make friends, but when it came to the usual crowds I found in school, I didn't really fit in. My lifestyle before I stopped drinking fit in with the revolutionaries and freaks, and even though a lot of my thought patterns are still similar to theirs, they still get high, and that makes us very unlike each other. I never could relate to the jocks, and the really straight people drove me up a wall. After passing through many lonely days, I found a few friends, a few kids to spend my free time with. My true friends have come to me through AA and they're the ones I feel truly are what friends should be.

Although my problems still make me feel empty at times, the major gaps in my life have been filled. My Higher Power reveals things to me as I need them. He does give me what I need, just not always what I want. My story won't end until my life ends, and with the grace of God, I'll be smiling. The key to this program is honesty, open-mindedness, and willingness to change. Just because you are reading this book, I know you have a touch of each. Remember, the only requirement for membership in the program is a desire to live a life free from the bondage of drugs.

Young, Sober, Free, and Grateful
I am seventeen with three years' sobriety and am not only free from the bondage of drugs but am free from the bondage of self-centeredness. What I've found is that I have choices, a choice in everything that comes my way. I am no longer a prisoner of drugs and as the title of this book says, I am young, sober, and free. *And* grateful!

CHAPTER 2

We've All Been Hung Up on God

"To whom it may concern: HELP!"
—Anonymous

Because of rejection, failures, heartaches, and those things that threaten you, will you turn your back on the chance given to you now? This is an opportunity to make your connection with the Powers of the Universe. You may decide not to—that's always one choice. But choosing to turn your back on this chance could be the same as signing your own death warrant. We ask you to finish reading this chapter and then decide what type of spiritual beliefs you will ascribe to or not.

Now think, how could God, any God, will that any should perish? We believe that for every hardship, every temptation, the Creative Forces of the Universe have provided a way out. For us, it is Twelve Step programs.

Lose the Devil's Triangle before It Loses You

Before going into the "God rap," it's important to speak of the spiritual foundation upon which our program is based. Because of the threefold nature of our disease, we see recovery as a threefold process too. Our addictive disease can be viewed as a triangle (see figure 1), a Devil's Triangle if you will, of physical compulsion and mental obsession (continued use despite negative consequences) built upon a base of self-centeredness. Recovery can be viewed as a triangle of physical abstinence and mental freedom (ability to choose) built upon a solid spiritual foundation of service to others.

Figure 1

**Devil's Addiction
Triangle**

**Clean & Sober
Recovery Triangle**

Recovery in only one area will not get us recovered, even a little bit. It's an all-the-way trip or no trip at all.

The God Rap

"But I've tried that God stuff before," we can hear you saying, "and it never worked!" So have we. In fact, most of us have investigated more than one religious or spiritual approach in all sincerity, striving to make sense of the world. It wasn't unusual to find us listening to Gregorian chants, on our knees in church, exploring the spiritual aspects of the martial arts, or reading *Embracing the Light,* always in an attempt to find "The Answer." To many of us, religious dogma has been a spawning ground of global conflict that hardly seemed fitting to answer the questions in our lives. Our Twelve Step program, on the other hand, represents a principled, loving way of life. And that difference is what we offer you. No dogma, no condemnation, just a simple, principled, loving way to be of service to our family, our community, and ourselves. This brings us to the Second Step and the "God rap."

Step 2: We came to believe that a Power greater than ourselves could restore us to sanity.

In order to stay clean and sober, we must seek a Power Source other than chemicals. You need a source you can rely on. People who discover this Power Source agree that it's an inside job. Osmosis won't work, neither will another person's concept of a Higher Power (HP) necessarily work for you for any length of time. In the beginning, you might try using your sponsor's HP. You might even use your home group or a sober high school as a Higher Power. But find a God of your understanding. Often, in seeking God, we addicts make our search more complicated (as we often do with all of life) than necessary. When we go to meet God, we want—if not expect—claps of thunder, burning bushes, an e-mail from heaven, or the God experience to resemble the euphoria of an E-bomb. But almost always, the experience of God is more down to earth, solid. Adam describes his experience this way:

> I was bummed out because I was trying to believe in God, praying like mad, and nothing was happening to me; I couldn't feel anything. I told a priest friend of mine about this and he said, "You are sitting there waiting for a voice to come out of the corner. Well, just maybe instead of coming out of the corner, the voice is coming out of me." From then on I knew God works through people, talks through people, and I was missing a lot because I was waiting for the voice from the corner. As time goes on, I see God all around me in people, places, and things.

It's okay to be rational and hesitant—the only mistake you can make in the Second Step is to be unwilling to seek your Spiritual Source. Cindy has a unique perspective:

> I spent weeks searching behind bushes, under trees, and just about everywhere for a Higher Power, but I found none. I expected a bolt of lightning or a burning bush and guess what? No go. I gave up my search and then it came. I don't care to say "God as we understand Him," but "God as we don't understand Him."

Insanity Is Doing the Same Thing Over and Over Again and Expecting Different Results

Only a few words need to be written about the second half of the Second Step: restore us to sanity. We don't mean insanity in a schizophrenic or psychotic sense. We mean the insanity of taking the first fix, pill, drink, tok, or line. Why, after we've proven again and again that it doesn't work for us, do we continue to pop that pill, smoke that crack, suck on that bottle? We call *that* insane. Our behavior, in that sense, is definitely unhealthy. However, it's only one symptom and isn't to be confused with the total addiction disease. Remember, chemical dependency isn't a symptom of mental illness. However, mental instability *is* often a symptom of chemical dependency. And this brings us to Step Three.

> **Step 3: We made a decision to turn our wills and our lives over to the care of God *as we understood Him.***

If you're asking, "How can I turn my will and my life over to God?" then you didn't read this the way it was written. We agree that you can turn your car keys (which you can see and touch) over to Mary (whom you can see and touch) but turning your will (that you can't see and touch) over to God (Whom you can't see or touch) would be impossible at this point. That's why you need to read the first four words, the magic words, "Made a decision to." We don't necessarily know how. All we do is make a decision to do it, just as we all can make a decision to go to India. We may not know how to go, whether by ship or plane, where to get the money, or how to obtain visas and passports. First, we make the decision; the execution of the decision comes later. This is our program: the decision first and the rest of the Steps are the execution. If you decide you want to take the Third Step, you've already taken it.

When You "Turn It Over," Let Go or You'll Be Upside Down

Many young people are afraid to make this decision, to turn it over to their Higher Power and let go of the reins. Their fears arise from different thought patterns:

- Maybe I'll never have anymore fun.
- I'm so young.
- Probably I'll be singing hymns with AA, CDA, and NA fanatics the rest of my life.
- I'll have to give up all the excitement of being young.
- Other young people will think I'm a nerd.

We've all faced these fears. To put it bluntly, though, we had to grow up and be realistic. Fun and excitement? Upon closer examination we saw that throwing up, stumbling around, fainting from dehydration, drive-by shootings, crack houses, car wrecks, constant terror of the cops, and screaming hysterical parents did not exactly spell fun and excitement. Singing hymns with fanatics? That's a cop-out. We found joyful, laughing people of all ages, ethnicity, and backgrounds at our meetings. Being called a nerd? We find that once we're clean and sober, others don't, and didn't, think about us nearly as often as we had thought.

God Helps Those Who Let Him Do His Job
Learning to let our Higher Power take over isn't as painful as it might appear at first. This is how Lori described it:

> I learned I had to move aside and let someone else take over my life. I had to pray for His will and be sure my motives weren't selfish or dishonest. Doing this was difficult because all my life I had been selfish, self-centered, and very dishonest. So all I could do was pray, "Thy will be done." And then strange things started to happen. I began feeling good inside after I had said the prayer. I started to pray more often, and His will started to happen. Before I knew it, I was eating my one-year cake at an AA meeting.

When we examine the basics of the first Three Steps, we see that it really is a simple program. Sometimes the simplicity escapes the complexity of our minds. Here are the first Three Steps in simple form:

I can't.
He can.
I think I'll let Him.

We can analyze and rationalize our way into or out of just about anything. So we ask you to stop the intellectual crap and just work the Steps. Judge the results later; don't try to understand it all now. You can't; you really can't. If we've learned nothing else, we have learned this about life: you can analyze it to death.

LEON'S STORY

*He thought that being strung out on heroin was the worst
thing possible, until he became an alcoholic.*

My name is Leon. I'm the fourth oldest in an African American family
of seven kids. My father and mother are God-fearing people who go to
church quite often. My mother's father died of alcoholism, as did his
brother who was my great-uncle. So did my mother's brother, my uncle
Neal. When I was a kid, I used to watch my uncle Neal drink, and I
would tell myself that that would never happen to me.

In high school I had a friend named Wade and we would get high
every day during first, second, and third periods. It was then that I
started smoking pot and liking it, but it had its drawbacks because my
teachers could smell it on my breath. One thing led to another, and in
my senior year I started drinking cold medicine with codeine in it. I remember that every morning at 9:00 I would meet Wade and we'd skip
class, go down to the drugstore, and buy two bottles of Robitussen A-C
cold medicine.

OTCs Don't Smell Like Alcohol

Buying over-the-counter (OTC) cold medicine was all right because it
didn't smell like alcohol, and when I went home high at night, my
mother never knew what was wrong with me. She'd ask why I was always so sleepy, and I would tell her, "Hey, Mom, I have to stay up late
studying, and besides, I work hard to get money." Because she couldn't
smell anything like alcohol, nothing more would be said.

Later, it dawned on me that because I liked both scotch and cough
medicine, it might be good to mix the two together. Well, let me tell
you, this was great! I found myself being able to do all the things I was
never able to do straight. I'd hear in school about how drugs would
make you lazy and hurt your body, but I thought that only happened

to weaker people. I worked eight hours a day, went to school for six more, and felt great. Now don't get me wrong, I couldn't run faster or jump higher, but any drugs that could turn me into a sexual giant and marathon man couldn't be all bad. Right? Well, my honeymoon with alcohol and cough syrup lasted right up to Christmas of that year.

I Woke Up with My Bed on Fire

On the Saturday night two weeks before Christmas, I was in my favorite bar (being tall and looking older than my age, no one ever asked for my ID), drinking shots of scotch with beer chasers, waiting for a friend of mine to bring me a couple bottles of Robitussen. He didn't come, and I was at the point of leaving when he came in. I quickly drank my two bottles of A-C, then continued drinking scotch. At about 1:00 A.M. I decided it was time to go home, because, for some reason, I wasn't getting high or drunk. About 1:30 A.M. I went home to go to bed, and the last thing I remember was sitting on the edge of the bed smoking a cigarette. About 3:00 A.M. I woke up with my bed on fire. I tried to put out the fire without my parents seeing the smoke, but I couldn't. My sister and mother both smelled the smoke and helped me put it out. That was the first time, so I thought, that alcohol and drugs got me in trouble.

Three days after a big drunk when I tried to stab some guy in a blackout, I decided that I should take more drugs and stay away from the alcohol. At school I continued to meet Wade, as usual. We had no plans to stop drinking cough medicine, but there had been a big drug bust in the recent past, and a law was passed that you had to be twenty-one to buy Robitussen and that you could only get it by a doctor's prescription.

After about two days of no Robitussen, Wade told me about a drug that was just like Robo, only it was more powerful and cost more. He called it "skag." That afternoon was to be my introduction to heroin. I had heard that this was a habit-forming drug and that it was hard to get. Well, it took us about ten minutes after we got out of school to find someone we could cop from.

I was still kind of worried about getting strung out on drugs, so I asked Wade about heroin's habit-forming effect. Wade's answer to me was, "You only get a habit if you do it every day, not once in a while like we would do." So I said, "Let's do it!" That first day I thought I'd never drink again because heroin didn't make me smell like alcohol did. I knew that this was my kind of high.

Had to Have a Skin Graft

After graduating high school, I got high on heroin every day for about a year, either before or after work. It was only by luck that I always made it to work—high or not high. One Friday evening, I took a light overdose of skag and fell asleep on a radiator. I woke up about two hours later with a skin burn about the size of a silver-dollar pancake. I worked around coal boilers the next night I went to work, and I told them I had burned my arm on a hot piece of coal at work.

Everybody except me was concerned about my arm. The company doctor said I'd have to have a skin graft operation and I did. My employer paid for 98 percent of all doctor bills, gave me sick pay for two weeks, vacation pay for two weeks, plus $350. Every penny went for drugs.

It wasn't long before I got fired. Three months after I lost the job, I got busted for selling drugs and was sent to a drug rehabilitation center for eight months. After getting out of rehab, I was busted again for drugs. At that point I told myself no more drugs and started drinking again.

Now, during this time, I had left the state, running from drug charges. My "new" life included alcohol, not other drugs. But my need for alcohol had turned into a twenty-four-hour thing. I remember talking with a friend who was an alcoholic, telling him that there wasn't any way in hell that I'd let alcohol interfere with my life or job. Yet, it all seemed to be happening. I told my friend Fran that the worst thing that could happen to a man was to be strung out on heroin. He just laughed and said, "I hope you never become an alcoholic." I don't know what ever happened to Fran, but he was right. Trying to stop drinking has been the hardest thing I've ever done, even harder than quitting heroin.

Losing Jobs and Using Women

After losing about twenty jobs and every woman I've ever loved because of alcohol, I decided it was time to get help, but from whom or where I didn't know. The first thing I did was call a hospital. They told me that I'd have to stay there from five to fourteen days, something I didn't want to do, so I said no. Next, I called an alcohol treatment center, but they asked for money down. They wanted to do a credit check and charge me $3,600. I felt they were just trying to rip me off, and anyway, if I had that kind of money, I would have been out getting drunk instead of wasting my time calling them.

The last and only place left I could think of was AA, so I gave them a call. I talked to a man named George who came and met me in a Laundromat. Later that night he took me to an AA meeting, an open speaker's meeting. At the close of the meeting, he told me more about the Twelve Steps of recovery and said that if I wanted to stop drinking, I could. He went on and told me about his own drinking career. I was impressed but not enough to stop drinking.

It took another two years of drinking for me to realize I was slowly dying, just like my uncle Neal. I had finally become what I never wanted to be, a man like my uncle. Not that I didn't love that man; I did. Like it or not, my grandfather was a drunk, Uncle Neal was a drunk, and now I'm the third-generation drunk in my family. Being at a point where I could no longer endure life, I knew I must stop drinking and taking drugs or kill myself, which I didn't have the courage to do, thank God.

The World Is Not My Prison but My Home

So my next answer was to call AA once again. I did that exactly one year and nine days ago. I now have a good job and have decided to go back to school. Family and friends want me to come back home. My father and I have learned how to talk to each other once more.

For the first time in my life, I've got something no one can take away from me and that something is me. For this change in my life, I'm grateful to AA. But I also thank God, for only He could have done what no others were able to do. This isn't the place where I have to be; it's the place where I am. The world is not my prison but my home. It is the road I must walk; the walking of it is called life. Because I will walk it only once, it's very important that I should walk it in some way that I can call my own.

CHAPTER 3

Escape to Reality

*"You can climb out of your bottle or fix or bag and notice
that the world isn't really worth hiding from."*
—Jimi

Some of the most important years of our lives were lost in the purple haze of addiction. We missed a lot of our natural growing-up processes or we experienced them behind that haze of mind-affecting chemicals. So actually we didn't grow up; as a result, we have some incredibly warped thinking and "attitude" that have not served us well. Without the escape of drugs, we must now deal with life on *life's* terms. The choice is ours. Either we deal with life or we pick up again. Nobody says it's going to be easy. But dealing with life *is* simple and can be done, providing we don't procrastinate or rationalize our way out of it. To put it off or make excuses for not working the remainder of the Steps would counteract any benefits we might expect from a clean and sober life. And the benefits are generally considered to be the Promises found on page 83 of the book *Alcoholics Anonymous*—often called the Big Book. Yes, we want the benefits and so we get to work.

Relief Lies in Two Four-Letter Words That Begin with *F*:
Steps Four and Five
In the first Three Steps, we prepared ourselves to work the next nine Steps. For this reason, Steps One, Two, and Three are considered the preparation, or foundation, Steps. The next six are the action Steps where we are expected *to do some work,* and the last three are maintenance Steps that keep us living by the principles we've learned. Step Four is the first action Step.

Step 4: We made a searching and fearless moral inventory of ourselves.

Anybody who's ever worked in a retail store or a fast-food restaurant knows what an inventory is. An inventory is really just a matter of counting and making a list of the particular things one has on hand. For members of Twelve Step programs, taking an inventory of ourselves doesn't have to be a big deal.

What we need to do is list the people, places, and things in our lives that we resent and that make us feel bad. Then we examine our reactions, in thought and deed, and see what we did that wasn't right. We don't list what others did that was wrong unless it helps clarify our own moral inventory. The wrongdoings of others isn't our concern here. Only ours is. We need to see what's good about our behavior and character and what isn't so good. We don't need to exaggerate or minimize— just state the facts and write the truth.

How to Work Step Four: *Begin*, the Rest Is Easy

How does one begin? You do it by sitting at your computer keyboard and typing or by inserting pencil in hand and applying to paper in front of you! Yeah, it's really that simple and any number of brilliant "yes, buts . . ." will not impress us, as our "yes, buts . . ." didn't impress the older members of the fellowships who walked us through the Steps. So get to work.

Although Step Four is fully explained in the book *Alcoholics Anonymous* (page 65) and in the NA basic text (page 27) and CDA text (page 49), we didn't always identify with the examples presented by members of another generation or era. So, we came up with examples of our own, using a four-column chart. Column one is where we list the person, place, or thing that we resent or have an attitude about. Column two is where we explain why it is a problem for us. Column three is how we reacted to it. The final column is where we list our character defect or the shortcoming revealed by our reaction. Here's an example of an inventory to help you get started:

Person, Place, or Thing I Resent(ed)	Reasons I Resent(ed)	My Reactions and My Behavior to This	Character Defect or Shortcoming Revealed
Chante and her best friend, Tracy	They laughed at me, and I think it's because Tracy said something about me and oral sex. I had wanted to hook up with Chante.	I spray-painted graffiti at the rec center about Chante.	Poor self-image Dishonesty Sexual insecurity Revengefulness Disregard of others
Joe and his big mouth	He acts tough, and I want people to see me as tough and be afraid to cross me too.	I brag that Joe just acts tough but that I could take him out if he crossed me.	Poor self-image False pride Insecurity Envy
Self	I stole from my neighbor who had always been nice to me. He paid me to mow his lawn, so I felt really low for taking his toolbox.	I called the neighbor a jerk to my parents, refused to mow his lawn anymore, and wouldn't look him in the eyes.	Greed Entitlement (theft) Poor self-image Disregard of others
Self and Joe	I let Joe talk me into carrying a gun because I had to prove I was as tough as him.	I stole a toolbox from the neighbor's garage to buy the gun.	"Attitude" Entitlement (theft) False pride People-pleasing
God	God let me be abused as a child.	I ran away a lot, fought with my mom and stepdad, cussed, was afraid often.	Insecurity "Attitude" Self-pity
My stepbrother, Jared	He always tries to get me to do more drugs: E-bombs, weed, acid. He says it's stupid that I went to treatment.	I tell him I get UAs so I can't do drugs, but it's just an excuse so he doesn't think I buy into recovery.	People-pleasing Dishonesty False pride Self-pity

Sex (oral)	I felt pushed into it and had to prove I was cool.	I pressured girls to "do me"—even ones I didn't like; used it to get drug money a few times; never told anyone.	Entitlement Follower (people-pleaser) Bullying Disregard of others
Other young people who are not druggies	They aren't addicts and don't have as complicated a life as I've created.	I put them down and act like they're nerds or geeks. When I'm around them, I show off and bully.	"Attitude" Envy Bullying Self-pity

Sometimes it can be rather difficult to understand how our *resentment* can reveal our defects. It may appear at first to be justified and reasonable. Take our friend Josh, for instance, who said, "I resent people not in recovery trying to get me to take drugs again." How could his resentment toward these fools reveal a shortcoming? You see, Josh is a bit envious that his friends can still do drugs—the addict in him wants to use too, and so the shortcomings revealed are envy and his fear of temptation.

To See What's Holding You Back, Look in the Fourth Step Mirror

Remember, being honest to the best of our ability in Step Four leads us to an honest Step Five. By the time we finish working Step Four, most of our self-centeredness should be staring us in the face. Boy, had we really thought a lot about our impact on society. Somehow we felt we were unique, so different, or so special. But it took only a little honesty to admit that the universe would run quite well without us. Rosemary described her progress through Steps Four and Five this way:

> When it came time for me to take my Fourth and Fifth Steps, I feared being honest. Some of the things I had done seemed so bad to me that if anyone found out about them, I was afraid I'd be locked up. I was sure people would never talk to me again. So it was a shock to find the person I took the Step

with had done many of the same things I did *and more*. It is such a relief to know that we aren't so special. Thinking about it beforehand, I almost got drunk, but learning I wasn't alone took a load off my back.

Step 5: We admitted to God, to ourselves, and to another human being the exact nature of our wrongs.

Spilling our guts out to another person doesn't sound like a picnic, but surprisingly, doing so provides a tremendous sense of relief. Let us caution you, though, please take this Step with someone whom you trust and who is unlikely to be hurt by what you disclose. We know your parents love you and at times you must feel very close, but doing a Fifth Step with them isn't a good idea. You might reveal too much for them to handle and create new pain and guilt. Also, as with boyfriends and girlfriends, might they not, in fits of anger, use something against you? The best choice is often a clergyperson specially trained to hear this Step. Your sponsor or an older member in the program who is not close to your parents are good choices too.

Step 6: We were entirely ready to have God remove all these defects of character.

The key here is willingness. Are we willing to have all the junk that was uncovered in the "F" Steps removed? Praying for willingness now is a start, yet it isn't enough. Many members mistakenly think this is a passive Step requiring no action on their part, just words. Not so. It's just as much an action Step as Four and Five. We act by *not* acting out and that's how we demonstrate our willingness in this Step. We stop any behavior connected to our character defects. If, for instance, we have identified revenge as a defect, then the next time we want to take revenge on someone, we simply *stop* the action of trying to get revenge. Do not tell the person's parents, turn him or her in, or poison the cat. How can we say we're truly willing to have our faults removed if we follow through on these inclinations to get even? *Stopping the negative behavior is true willingness.* The defect may still be there, eating us up, but we *act* willing and then we progress to Step Seven.

Step 7: We humbly asked Him to remove our shortcomings.

Wow! These shortcomings have been constant, close companions for years; they're comfortable and "easy" for us, a whole lot easier than a way of life that demands mature responses and accountability. If our shortcomings and defects are removed, then we can't blame our parents, the school, or society at large for our troubles. We might have to become responsible ourselves! Look at that word *responsible:* response-able. Who is "able" to "respond" better to our lives than us? Having our shortcomings removed means we're placed in a position of being responsible for our own actions and then acting on principle.

We no longer can use self-will trips, saying such things as, "Well, what do you expect? I'm sick" or "Sorry, I've always had a problem with _____ because of my rotten childhood." Nobody in the real world cares if you're sick or had a rotten childhood. They don't care about you getting in touch with your "inner child" or your "inner juvenile delinquent." They simply don't want you disrespecting them, using them, and causing trouble. And if you disrespect others, you are ultimately disrespecting yourself. Suzi described the freedom she felt once her Higher Power began this transformation in her life:

> My newfound freedom is hard to express. I like myself today, even love myself. I have respect for myself and others. I found out that I'm not the stupid, fat, ugly, loud, obnoxious girl that I once thought I was. I'm becoming a beautiful, caring whole woman who is able to feel, touch, hold, and contribute. I no longer feel empty inside.

We find it to be a "release from the bondage of self" to let God remove these defects of character. How is this done? Proceed to Step Eight and as you work your way through the remaining Steps, your Higher Power will be working His or Her way through your shortcomings.

Step 8: We made a list of all persons we had harmed and became willing to make amends to them all.

You can write most of this list by referring back to the Fourth Step. It's important, however, not to justify your behavior and conveniently leave names off the list because their behavior was worse than yours. It doesn't matter if Jane Doe stole your boyfriend; that's no excuse for telling one "little" lie about her. If you harmed her, you harmed her, and her name goes on the list. By completing the list, each of us affirms our *willingness,* and then we go immediately to Step Nine.

Step 9: We made direct amends to such people wherever possible, except when to do so would injure them or others.

Here we meet the misdeeds of our past, as we would have others meet us with their wrongdoings. Ask yourself, did you steal money? It needs to be paid back, even if it takes years to do so. Destroy property? Likewise, you must pay for the damage you caused.

Did you gossip or tell lies? Although your words cannot be taken back, you can take action to change their effect, regardless of your image. You admit the wrong impressions you spread about and set the record straight. You talk to the people you said the dishonest words to, not necessarily the one you said it about. Here's an example of how one girl, Jeanette, did this:

> I had dissed a professor in college, accusing her of racism, to anyone who would listen. She gave me my one and only C in all of my college classes, and I felt it was a prejudice on her part because I was a straight-A student. When it came time to make amends, though, I knew I had to address this. I told my

sponsor I was making an appointment to apologize to her and my sponsor asked, "What for? To dis her to her face?" My sponsor explained that unless the professor knew I had bad-mouthed her to others, I shouldn't hurt her by telling her what I had said. I needed to undo the verbal disrespect with the ones I had talked to.

Apologies, Amends, Action

We don't find it necessary to plunge into lengthy explanations or corn-ball confessions. Open, direct admissions of wrongs and what we intend to do about them is sufficient. Don't confuse apologies for amends, though. An amends might include an apology but they're not the same. Apologies are simply words, but an amends Step is an *action* step and it requires us *to do something*. We must repair any damage we have done, whether it's in energy, time, or money. We must tell the injured party that we intend *not* to repeat the behavior and how we intend to make it right with them, and then do it.

We find that many of our amends are made by living this new way of life. We don't limit ourselves to saying, "Sorry, Mom, that I was such a screw-up." We *show* her we are changing, and that is living our way through an amends.

Helter-Skelter Amends

In our quest for progress, we oftentimes unthinkingly involve or incriminate others and thereby harm them. We need to *think* and ask for guidance before making helter-skelter amends, as Jeanette's story (above) shows. We should admit *our* wrongdoings, not the wrongdoings of others. This is a good time to go to your sponsor and have a thorough discussion about these matters. Don't incriminate friends or strangers from your dope-dealing days, and don't "confess" things to your family that may cut them to the core. They have hurt enough while watching your disease progress; they shouldn't have to hurt again while watching you take your Steps toward recovery.

Likewise, we're very careful to approach those we're making amends to, thinking only of what we've done and cleaning up our side of the street. We push aside the wrongs they've done to us. This Step isn't about them; it's about us. As hurt or angry as we've been with them, we pray for guidance and make our amends only when we know we can focus on ourselves, for ourselves, and do this Step properly. It would not do to start accusing them of all their wrongdoings, excusing your behavior with, "Well, if you hadn't done thus and such in the first place, then I wouldn't have done _____ but I'm sorry." That isn't a proper amends. So get together with your HP before you begin.

A Fear Faced Is a Fear Erased

Once the past is cleared, our fears of the future begin disappearing. Living in the *here and now* proves to be an exciting, challenging path to follow. After all, today is all we can ever experience at any given time. We're no longer bummed out by the there and then or overwhelmed by the where and when. Remember, "now" reversed is "won."

Our path becomes a part of a process and we begin to see rhyme and reason and even gain trust in the process. We begin to feel like living and become a part of the great flow of life. Some of us even find ourselves eventually saying things like, "I'm a grateful alcoholic and addict," when gratitude for this disease was an idea that had totally confused us before.

In the light of our expanding consciousness, it dawns on us that life is a very happy and secure reality after all.

LEE'S STORY
His conversations with other people were mostly
interruptions with his inner dialogue.

Part One, Early Childhood

"Oscar Lee—Oscar Lee—Get up and get in the kindling and coal. You didn't do it last night, so get up and go do it and hurry up. You never do anything you're supposed to and—"

Thut!

"Okay! Okay! You don't have to throw a butcher knife. That stuck in my pillow! You're crazy!"

"Don't you talk to me that way or I'll get the razor strap!"

(Crack! Crack! That's Grandma's neck. Whap! Whap! That's her arms. Thud! That's her wrinkled face. I hate her. I hate her. I'm going to run away.)

"Oscar Lee. You got that kindling? Bring it here and quit messing round. Now you get out there and feed and water those rabbits—and don't you forget any either. You left a cage open yesterday, and that old brown doe got away and that old rusty dog had to catch her. You never do anything right no how. . . ."

(Goddamn rabbits—Goddamn Grandma—Goddamn everything!)

Part Two, High School

"Lee, what makes you think you can walk out of here, be gone for three weeks, and stroll back in as if nothing had happened?"

(Oh boy, big deal!)

"Mister, you have one more chance in school. Do you hear me?"

"Yes, sir, I'll be good! (How many times have I heard this crap, "One more chance"? I'm sick of it. "This is your last chance"—bullshit.) Yes, sir, I hear ya. I'll be good."

* * *

(It was Marylin's mother. She transferred Marilyn so she wouldn't be around me. Why can't people just stay out of my life—leave me alone?)
"Marilyn, I guess this is good-bye. I have another girl pregnant, and I guess I'm gonna have to marry her—I guess it don't matter anyway. You're going with someone else. I love you. . . ."

"Lee, I think I know how to solve this. You wouldn't have to marry her if you were already married to someone else—*me*."

"Do you mean it? Would you marry me?"

* * *

"Hey, Lee, don't hog that hooch! Someone else might want some of it. Hand it back up here or I'll kick your ass."

"You and who's army?" (Betty's pregnant; I'm kicked out of the house; no job and Marilyn don't love me. Running away with some guy for three days to Utah. I don't want her back—I want her dead. I want me dead. To hell with it.)

Part Three, Age Twenty
(Goddamn! Three and a half years in the army, getting discharged in New York, waking up in Washington D.C., thinking I was in Chicago—finding a job, a rooming-house room. I haven't touched a girl in months. Where is it all heading? I feel like I'm fourteen. I wish I had a woman—any goddamned woman. I should have married that girl in Germany. What was her name? . . .)

"Gimme a shot and a beer."

(I'll get cleaned up and go to a nice restaurant and I'll meet a really nice chick—a lean, lanky blonde, nicely proportioned with nice clothes. She'll be really nice to me and I'll take her to her apartment and it'll be all real feminine and we'll talk and have another drink and dance and then we'll go to bed. . . .)

"Another one."

(If I had a model A with a Chrysler 300 and dual carburetors and a four speed and dual glass packs, I'd be running a hundred miles an hour

and playing the radio full blast and Marilyn and a girlfriend would see me streak by. Marilyn would think she saw me and . . .)

"Another one."

(If that big guy came over here and said something to me I'd say, "Why don't you shut up?" and he'd take a swing at me and I'd throw up my left arm to block the blow and I'd grab him by the shirt and I'd throw him over my right hip and he'd crash into the juke box and . . .)

"Yeah, another one."

(I'm really a lot different person than anyone knows—I'm smarter and tougher and I can draw and nobody knows any of that. Nobody really knows me at all. They think I'm a coward. If I had a chance, I'd show 'em.)

"Yeah, one more. . . . Okay, okay, I'm leaving anyway."

(I need a girl—I'm gonna hide in this alley and if a woman comes by, I'm gonna grab her and pull her into the alley and make her have sex with me, but I'm not gonna hurt her—I want her to like me. . . . If she were in pink lipstick . . . gotta get home, where's my key? Gotta get up in three hours. . . .

What the hell 'm I doin' in this water? I'm all wet. God I'm sleeping in the tub! Gotta get out of these wet clothes and get to work. Gotta get some coffee! Wonder if anyone saw me sleeping in the tub with my clothes on. Wher'd I go last night?)

"Sorry I'm late—I didn't have bus fare. I had to walk."

"What's that stuck in your eyebrows?"

(My God, it's puke. I got sick last night in the tub.)

"Why are you always broke the next day after pay day? You should budget. I'll make you a deal. If you come to work on time every day for five days in a row, I'll give you a nickel raise. Soon I won't be able to afford to pay you and then I'll go to work for you."

Part Four, Age Twenty-One

"Oscar L. B., you're charged with being drunk and disorderly and resisting arrest. How do you plead?"

"Guilty, your Honor."

"The man ahead of you has been in this jail over forty times and the man behind you over ninety times. From the condition you were in when you came in, I have no reason to believe you won't be back. I sentence you to life on the installment plan. You can serve it any way you like, ten, thirty, ninety days at a time or in larger quantities. There is an alternative—if you're interested; go through the door in the back of the courtroom."

"God, grant me the serenity to accept the things I cannot change, the courage to change the things I can, and the wisdom to know the difference. Hi, I'm Bill, and I'm an alcoholic. I come down here every morning to pay the debt to the man that helped me when I got out. Alcoholics Anonymous can show you a way of life that can make it possible for you to live without liquor and jails. If you want what we have and are willing to go to any lengths to get it, it works."

(Man does that air smell good. Green grass! Trees! Birds! God it's good to be alive. Four days behind bars can give a man a different outlook. No more booze! I'll go to their meetings and live up to the conditions of the probation.)

* * *

(Where am I? What's goin' on?")
". . . so I went to AA and I haven't had a drink since."

(I'm in an AA meeting! How'd I get here? Oh, my head! I wonder who sent me. Where have I been? What have I done?) "Oh no, I don't have anything to say." *(I don't want to drink. I want to work and get rich and fall in love. Maybe I can get Marilyn back, or maybe I can fall in love with some farm girl and have a nice house. . . .)*

Part Five, Growing Up
(I'm in a liquor store! How the hell did I get here? I don't remember walking here. I don't want to drink!) "Uh, I'll just have a pack of Pall Malls." *(Better get to the AA club. Maybe Abe'll be there!)*

"Abe, I just found myself in a liquor store and I don't remember the last several blocks. I'm scared. I just got a pack of cigarettes and got my butt down here. Have you ever heard of anybody doin' that?"

"Not that, exactly, but I have heard of people having delayed reactions to alcohol and that could be what it was. You're going to need God's help if you're gonna stay sober."

"Abe, I don't know how to pray. I'm not sure I believe in God. Maybe good, but I don't know about God!"

"I didn't either. I just talked to Him like I do to you and slowly I started getting answers. I have come to rely on Him over the years."

(God, whoever You are—whatever You are—if you exist, I need help!)

"Lee, I've known you for almost a year now, and I think we're pretty good friends. Being blind, I can't tell how old you are. You must be about my age from your story. I'm fifty-one."

"No, Abe, I'm only twenty-three. I've just got a lot of miles. . . ." (Does *he know I've been lying? Does he know what I'm really like? Would he still like me if he really knew?*)

Part Six, Learning about the Fellowship

(Why don't I just walk out on the whole thing and go find Marilyn? Maybe I was so screwed up when I was in Chicago, I just imagined that she was a lesbian. God knows I've imagined an awful lot of things. I don't know what to believe. Well, I can believe some things—AA has helped me stay sober. I couldn't do that on my own. I'm sure that I want to make my living in art—making signs anyway. It's a good thing I can go to the AA club and release all my frustrations.) "Hi, Henrietta, whendja get outta jail?"

"Hi, you rotten kid. Why don't you go back home?"

"I don't have a home. You gonna let me move in with you?"

"Not on your life!"

"If you're not nice to me, I'm gonna throw your coat in the trash again."

"You're gonna pay the cleaning bill this time too."

"Good morning, Bill. Sausage 'n' eggs and bowl of snot!"

"You really know how to improve everyone's appetite, don't you? Why don't you eat at home and let everyone else enjoy eating here?"

"I'm just trying to spread joy and love."

"Why don't you wash your hair?"

"You just wish you had some!"

"Oh, you're rotten."

"Thank you."

"I thought you were going to Phoenix."

"I was but I couldn't afford to get to the edge of town."

"If I had your talent, I'd be a millionaire."

"Yeah, and if I could hang on to money the way you do, I'd own Denver."

"Lee, your breakfast is up."

"Okay, thanks, Bill. This looks almost good enough to eat. Hi, Russ, where ya been, in jail?"

"No, I have to stay out so I can pay your bail."

"How's your wife and my kids?"

"You want 'em back?"

"No thanks, I can't handle the ones I got."

"I thought you were going to Phoenix."

"I ran out of money before I got out of town."

Part Seven, Today

(God, I'm powerless over alcohol and my life is unmanageable. You can restore me to sanity and today I'm gonna let You. Please direct my thinking today, especially that it be divorced from self-pity, dishonesty, self-seeking motives, jealousy, and lust. You know, God, the jealousy is gone. I don't know what You're doing with the lust but that's Your business. I guess I could be a little more cooperative by not buying the dirty books and stuff like that. I offer myself to You to build with me and to do with me as You will. Relieve me from the bondage of self that I may better do Your will. I guess You have done that. I seem to be effective in helping other people and I seem to add some happiness to other people's lives. I know I make a lot of people laugh and some really like to see me. Take away my difficulties that victory over them may bear witness to those I would help of Your love. I guess I have been doing Your will even though I was all screwed up. I didn't drink or kill myself, and I've learned to laugh both at myself and with

others. My kids love me and my wife and I are getting along better. Shit, I don't daydream as much as I used to. I may not look like a hell of a miracle to other people but I sure do to You and me.)

"Young man, how can you purport to work a spiritual program with that vulgar mouth?"

"I just do."

CHAPTER 4

Don't Stop Now

"There is nothing I cannot do in God's world; I only limit myself
by living in my world with all my limitations."
—Julia J.

About this time in working the Steps, doubts creep in, unanswerable questions plague us, and we begin to wonder if we're actually moving forward or if this whole sobriety thing is just one giant step forward and two steps back. Our bodies are back in shape, our lives are somewhat intact, and that hard drive in our head has been defragmented and is functioning fine. Beware. Lurking in the virus vault in the back of your brain remains your addictive voice, ever ready to run its script on you should it get an opening.

We've found ourselves saying things like:

- "I'm okay now, so I can hang out with an old bud rather than hit a meeting."
- "I did enough work in treatment and enough is enough. I don't have to be a fanatic about all this working the Steps stuff."

You may even have some well-meaning—but clueless—adults in your life telling you that you're "too young to be a *real* alcoholic or addict." These thoughts are akin to the addiction virus breaking out of the vault and worming its way through your head. Sooner or later your system is going to crash. Check your thoughts with the best anti-addiction virus program around—your Higher Power, your sponsor, your counselor—and/or share them at a meeting. Julia went almost five years without running her anti-addiction software before her system crashed:

> At five years sober, I was being told by some that I was a miracle and to be admired and by others that I had better work a program or I would drink again for sure. I decided to err on the side of caution and asked a woman with two years to sponsor me; even though she had less clean and sober time than I did, I thought she had more inside. She had me do a written First Step and I did; then she wanted to talk about Steps Two and Three. I imagined that because I had had God pounded into my head, I didn't need to look at these Steps. Later, I found out that was exactly *why* I needed to look at them. I mumbled something about doing a Fourth Step and stopped talking to her. A year and a half later, I took that first drink without any thought about what might happen and then chased the ensuing fear away with ideas like I was an adult now and it would be different. It was different all right; it got worse!

Keep Stinking Thinking in the Virus Vault

It shocks us with what ease our heads get into what is called "stinking thinking." We almost always begin with some b.s. rationalization for exercising self-will. *We want what we want when we want it.* What rationalization means is that we try to give a reason that sounds good for getting what we want when we want it. So we do a form of mental gymnastics to justify why we really *have* to have a particular thing, or *have* to go there, or *must* be with that person—instead of working Steps and asking for guidance. Most of the time, the reasons we make up sound good at the time. But that doesn't make them true and our gut will tell us so, if we listen.

Stinking thinking is the best reason for moving forward from the foundation Steps (1 through 3) to the action Steps (4 through 9) and continuing with the maintenance Steps (10 through 12), because the Steps *keep us honest* and keep the addiction virus in the vault instead of worming its way through our brains.

Step 10: We continued to take personal inventory and when we were wrong promptly admitted it.

One thing you can always count on is change. Because our world is changing and we're changing, we must keep striving to grow or we stagnate. We can do this by taking a daily inventory that tracks these changes and our reaction to them. Jill explained her experience with the Tenth Step this way:

> I used to always go through phases when I really felt down and never knew why. This drove me up a wall, made me hyper, and then I'd want to escape. Through my daily inventories, I can sort out my feelings, detect growing resentments, and keep a space cleared for contact with my HP.

Julia uses the Tenth Step for quick self-evaluations for the positive as well as the negative:

> When I was younger, my dad had a bunch of strokes and my mom also had health problems. I took responsibility for it and I felt guilty and less-than. From then on I had an automatic re-action when anything happened that I was the wrong one and the guilty party. The maintenance Steps keep me balanced.

So for Julia, Step Ten is also a way to see where she is *not* wrong and is *not* to blame. Doing daily inventories keeps her clear.

Three Ongoing Inventories
We've learned that the program implies there are three types of continuing inventories:

- **The Quickie** (Step Ten): Here we look at our motives for what we do to make sure our house is in order. For example, "Why did I just snap at my mom? That's not recovery behavior. I'll apologize right now."

- **The Daily Review** (Step Eleven): Here we review our day before going to sleep and make sure there are no leftover guilt feelings warning us that something needs to be tended to. For example, "I'm bothered that I told that newcomer I couldn't offer a ride. Because it bothers me, I probably should do just that. I will call in the morning and agree to take her to a meeting tomorrow."

- **The Retreat Inventory** (Steps Four and Ten): This is a more thorough self-examination that we take at retreats or following major life events when the daily or quickie won't address our changing needs. For example, "I broke up with Tanya and I really loved her. I was tempted to use again without her. I better take another inventory—maybe on sex and love. I'll talk to my sponsor."

Our thoughts have to be constructive and honest. Each day, an individual meets his or her own self—in the physical, the mental, or the spiritual phase of one's personal experience. And for our life experience to be one of growth, we must be honest, constructive, and steady.

> **Step 11: We sought through prayer and meditation to improve our conscious contact with God *as we understood Him*, praying only for knowledge of His will for us and the power to carry that out.**

Through prayer we talk to our Higher Power and through meditation we listen. In our spiritual program we learn to do both. Not of ourselves alone can we accomplish the transformation of our lives. No human power, philosophy, or health food supplements can replace Divine intervention and direction. Nor can we receive such complete love and joy from any other source.

Prayer

The goal of this book is not to teach you how to pray. You may have a spiritual advisor, a sponsor, a religion, or a philosophy of your own. It is only our intent to share with you how liberating communication with your Spiritual Source is. Some people find that ritualized prayer—such as saying the Rosary every day or getting on their knees in the morning and expressing gratitude—works well for them. Some people are more comfortable talking to God on the way to school or work in a casual, everyday exchange. Here's what works for Joy:

> I call my God a "partner," because I can understand the idea of a partner a lot better than I can understand the idea of God as a father. My partner only expects honesty of me, wanting me to tell Him the truth, no matter how rough that truth might be. He runs the show because he knows more than I do. I find the program is not the bitch I thought it would be, because my partner never lays anything on me that He and I can't handle together. It's a good feeling to know that my partner goes with me everywhere—even to school. If things get rough at school, I just go anyplace where I can be by myself and have a little chat with Him. He comes through every time!

We know of many program families that keep a stack of meditative books on their kitchen tables. Before the evening meal or maybe at Sunday brunch, each member of the family takes a book and reads the daily passage, praying as a family. Prayer, in whatever form, is an opportunity to deepen our bonds with God. The only guidelines for effective prayer are that you offer it from a genuine desire to know the will of your Higher Power and to show gratitude. If you use prayer to ask for something, make sure it's for the benefit and highest good of those in your life and not for selfish gain.

Prayer is often thought of in terms of receiving something from God. We find, however, that a great spiritual exercise is to *give* something to God. Instead of asking what God can do for us, we find it's better to ask what we can do for God. "What would you have me do today?" This way we're offering to let God make our decisions for the day or in the situation we are praying about.

Meditation

The actress Lily Tomlin once asked, "Why is it that when I talk to God it's called prayer and when God talks to me it's called schizophrenia?" Although some people don't believe that Divine Will can actually come directly to us—thinking that when we "hear" or "know" the will of our Spiritual Source, we must be crazy—we know this isn't so. Yes, we understand that some people suffer from illnesses where they hear voices and experience things they believe are God. Additionally, we've all had experiences with the drug-induced/withdrawal-induced hallucinations. Those confused states do require professional help. Yet we easily distinguish our connection to God from pathological breaks from reality. A loving, guiding Higher Power never *insists* we do anything—there are no *musts* or *demands;* we are only offered loving choices. With Divine influence, we don't become manic or obsessive. The word *serenity* comes to mind. God brings us peace and solidness, not euphoric, panic-stricken, or crazed states of being.

Listening to our Higher Power and being guided by the Divine within is called meditation. The most popular form of meditation consists of relaxing in a quiet place, letting the limbs go limp, and trying to clear the mind. Yet, this isn't always the ideal form of meditation for the energetic young person. Three distinct types of meditation can be used in our program:

- **Mental meditations** include concentration, grounding, group meditation, guided meditation, mantras, meditation on thoughts, mindfulness, noting meditation, and spiritual practice in daily life.
- **Sensory meditations** include art as meditation, breath meditation, mandalas, music and chants, sensory awareness, and visualization meditation.
- **Movement meditations** include rituals, dance meditation, martial arts, sports meditation, and walking meditation.

All forms of meditation require concentration and use rhythmic patterns of some sort. This helps still our everyday frustrations and focuses our attention. Meditation is a great tool for getting to know ourselves, seeing life more objectively (without the chatter of our inner spoiled child), and creating a space for guidance.

Just as we all have different learning styles (some learn when they see things, some are hands-on learners, some learn through reading, and others through hearing), we all have meditative styles that suit us best. You might be the intellectual type best served by mental meditations (MM). Such meditations are designed to discipline your mind through concentration, teaching you not to skip from one topic to another. You grow through observation of your personal psychological processes. MMs help us discern the types of distractions that snag our attention. Those distractions might include worries, fears, or sexual fantasies. With MM we learn about our values and mental habits.

You may be a better learner through your senses. In sensory meditations (SM), we allow the senses (touch, sight, sound, psyche, perception) to stretch beyond our everyday habits, emotional and mental preferences, and other routines. We allow our senses to simply sense things without our input. We do not control *but allow*. With the breath, we allow it to occur in its natural cadence and depth. Envision as we inhale, the energy of light coming into our bodies. As we exhale, we feel the energy circulating throughout our bodies. With our eyes, we gaze at an object—real or in our minds—that symbolizes beauty or humility or some other principle we're practicing. Although our gains through SM are much the same as with mental meditations, we also perceive more accurately; we increase our understanding of the physical body; we learn to live in the moment.

On the other hand, you may be very energetic and learn best in the physical, "hands-on" style of movement meditations. Movement is a means of self-discovery. We delve into our bodies in order to find something to express. In this search, we perceive elements that we didn't know previously—different emotions, attitudes, and thoughts. Thus we learn more about our hearts and souls as our bodies become energized through movement, and we understand that any action—including the actions associated with violence—can be used for the purpose of growth. In the martial arts, the energy of the conflict, rather than muscles, is used as a means of resolution. The attitude is detachment and serenity; the intent is to settle rivalry and conflict harmlessly, whether it's an inner or outer battle.

In Step Eleven, we confront the forces that would divert our attention from living by principle. We gain insight, access, and connection to our Spiritual Source. James Harvey Stout wrote in his Internet book the "World of Meditation" that through meditation, "We examine the 'will.' When we willfully direct our attention toward an object, we can study the nature of the will as it responds to the many stimuli which would try to divert it to serve their own needs." And so we use prayer and meditation to learn about our will and how to align it with that of our Creator.

It Works If You Work It

And finally, we never forget the morning routine of our prayer and meditation. We seek the protection from our Spiritual Source each morning before leaving for work or school. We ask, "God, please help me to stay clean and sober today." There is more to this program than just not shooting up, getting high, or rolling. We no longer concern ourselves with the world of drugs but cling to the world of recovery. Our new life is confined only by the limitations we allow. Each of us should be aware that a sound personal program—balanced in body, mind, and soul—offers far more potential than any of the trips we have come off in the past.

SUZANNE'S STORY
"Your daughter's smoking pot. Congratulations!"

I grew up in Texas. I have a family full of alcoholics and addicts, which is just grand. My mom is sober and I don't think she was ever an addict, just drank a lot for a while. My parents were divorced when I was nine. My mom said they married for lust, not for love. So, in our family there would be lots of fighting, sex, leaving, coming back—abuse of all sorts, including physical, mental, emotional, and sexual.

My grandparents and aunt didn't live too far. My aunt drank and smoked pot. The whole family drank. It was like the elephant in the middle of the room. Everyone drank and smoked pot and my grandfather abused pain pills that he started on from a hurt back twenty years prior. Mom used to drink a lot too. The drug abuse was so obvious, but no one talked about it.

After my mom got a promotion and we moved to Kansas, my dad just dropped us out of his life. We were in Kansas only a short time when I began hurting myself. I never took anything out on anyone else. I collected it inside—the shit from my dad and all my unhappiness. I started by beating my arms and legs, and then I covered up the bruises, telling lies about why I wore long sleeves all the time. It would be ninety degrees outside, sweat would be trickling down my neck, and I would tell my mom, "I'm cold," and she would say, "You're weird," and that was that. As soon as I started shaving my legs, I discovered razors. I turned from hitting myself to cutting myself. Then I really had to act weird to hide it.

At school I didn't feel comfortable and just covered up and lied about everything. If they asked me where my dad was, I'd say something like, "Oh, he's an astronaut and in space right now." Actually it was me who was in space. I was old enough to know better than to lie, but I did it anyway.

My Thirteenth-Birthday Present: Addiction

When I began middle school, my older brother got into drugs real heavy. It seemed to be our birthright from the hippie lifestyle we grew up in. We also celebrated Jewish holidays, which included heavy drinking and was fairly well accepted. The first time I got high was my thirteenth birthday; it was a gift from a friend.

My mom worked at a temple and wanted to live closer, so we moved within ten minutes of the temple. With that move and beginning my ninth-grade year at school, I gravitated to the grunge scene and wanted to be identified with the outcasts. We skipped school, stole, smoked a lot of pot, and I began cutting really bad. There was not a time that trails of red crusty marks did not marble my arms and legs. I didn't want anyone to know, so I hid it. Yet I needed to *feel* the rush of hurting myself to escape from reality, so I would scratch at my cuts through my clothing while I was at school. I loved the feeling of numbness but hated that it was followed by guilt and shame.

My biggest outlet, besides cutting, was drugs and alcohol. Drinking and drugging were my best friends. I thought it should be written down somewhere that "Drugs and alcohol make you happy." It worked for me.

Grounded for the Rest of My Life

Finally, my mom caught me smoking pot because a friend's mom came to her office and told her, "Your daughter's smoking pot. Congratulations." My mom got pissed. Of anybody, I thought my mom wouldn't care. When I was younger, she *helped* my brother grow weed, so I thought our family was cool with weed. Now she changed on me and thought it was bad! I was grounded for the rest of my life and she made me go to her work with her every day after school.

We fought all the time, as she kept control of me and stayed alert to see if I was smoking. Since I couldn't smoke pot because my mom was going to give me drug tests, I had to switch gears. I knew that at the temple there were many huge parties and celebrations. Jews like to drink and eat. Lots of wine flowed. So I'd go there every day after school like mom wanted, and I played the part of a good little secretary—

I even got paid. But I took a lot of breaks and went into the kitchen and drank all the hard liquor I could get in me. I stole it and brought it home and hid it in the closet.

Finally I went to my mom and told her I needed help. She said, "Okay, I'll call a counselor." "No," I protested, "I don't need another counselor." They never did shit anyway; I just lied to them. A week later I took a bottle of Jack Daniels to school in my backpack and got really drunk. I had been drunk at school a lot but never brought it with me because of the zero-tolerance thing. In gym, two of my friends got drunk with me. Anyway, we were caught. The bottle had been "hidden" in a tampon box but was spotted because it didn't fit. Anyway, we were sent to the office and suspended. I lied and tried to tell them we just found it, but the school police officer came and read us our rights.

At Least I Got to Get Drunk

My only thought was, "My mom's going to kill me." I didn't care about getting in trouble, getting kicked out of school, or getting read my rights, *just my mom killing me.* But I tried to look at the bright side—at least I got to get drunk.

My mom called a treatment center and told me it was just for kids who had problems. I didn't want to go to rehab because I didn't do drugs—*I wasn't a drug addict.* So just before I went, I dropped some acid—a lot. It was a bad trip; the flames of hell consumed me. So I rather welcomed rehab at that point. Still, I lied about my use at intake. But Mom insisted I needed help and told them I was doing a lot more than what I let on. So they admitted me into inpatient.

It took me a while to open up, but I finally began talking about my cutting. I opened up about my father and what he did to me. I even cut in rehab and started bawling in this one group. It had been hidden for seven years and now it was out. They told me to tell my mom, so I called her. Mom told me she already knew and just wanted me to get better. I got on the appropriate medication and my whole life changed. In therapy I was able to let go of so much. My relationship with my mom and brother improved too.

Back at school, it didn't go as well. My friends would pull out a joint and wave it under my nose and say, "This is really good weed, free weed," then snatch it back and say, "But you can't have any!" The crisp smell of a joint taunted me. My "friends" coupled with over-whelming emotions became too much. For years I had numbed out and now I actually had to feel everything and I couldn't take it. So I de-cided, *no more.*

Sober High (School That Is!)

This compelled me to seek another way. The new way turned out to be a sober high school. It was here that I began working a real recovery program. I don't think I would have done it on my own, but at Com-munity High, it's one of the prerequisites for admission. Here they in-sisted on doing ninety meetings in ninety days—I did. Meetings weren't my first choice, but I was desperate to get into this school. They said, "Get a sponsor." I got a sponsor. More than one, even. Members in the Twelve Step groups said to take what you wanted and leave the rest, and I took that too literally. I got a bunch of different sponsors because anytime I didn't like what one said, I got another one!

Cutting and Chemicals or Serenity?

At about one year, I was getting into relapse mode. Real icky. My cut-ting began again. Meetings fell to about three every two weeks. The fa-cade I presented didn't work as well as I'd liked. I got a lot of shit put on me. Then I realized that *I wanted* recovery, really wanted it. The seren-ity they spoke of in meetings and the promises of freedom beckoned me. I wanted the peace the program brought, not the numbness of cutting and chemicals. So I went back to meetings, got a real sponsor, and started working the Steps in earnest. I really want this way of life.

Even though the school isn't supposed to be my program, for a while it was. I owe my sobriety to my sober high school. I am now work-ing with my sponsor and approaching the Fourth Step I so dreaded. I know that this way of life is better for me and I choose to work this Step rather than use. I could make lists of all that's going well—I get up every morning and pray to a Higher Power that I love. I have good, solid relationships. I used to say drugs and alcohol made me happy, but they were a facade—not real. Today I see getting high as numbness, not happiness. Today's "sad" is an okay sad, and all my emotions are valid.

There and Aware

I was in Houston not long ago visiting family around Thanksgiving. I slipped outside at the break of dawn to pray and at first couldn't feel the presence of God. So I centered myself and noticed this pure and powerful moment in the early morning. Birds warbled, fresh air wafted over me, and the brightness of the day revealed itself and feelings of love floated in and around me. I was so *there and aware,* a point I could never have reached before. It's called a spiritual experience. I had been jealous of those with spiritual experiences before. Now I know this direction I'm going in is great. What a great Thanksgiving and at the beginning of the holiday, it was just what I needed.

Of course, I have people I had to let go because they're in active addiction. And recovery isn't perfect; there's pain in sobriety too, but this is my life and I love it.

So, Mom, now your daughter is sober. Congratulations!

CHAPTER 5

S.O.S.: Saving Our Selves

"I used to worry about whether I'd be any help. What should I say?
I found if I just turned it over to my HP and let Him use me as a
channel, things worked out and I felt good about it. I'm not
going out to save them, but to save me."
—Gary

This chapter on Step Twelve embodies the foundation of our continuing sobriety by having us do service work and carry the message to others. So why do we call this "Saving Our Selves" if we'll be learning to work with others? In our workshops, when we were brainstorming the title of this chapter, we came up with a number of pretty good titles such as

Reaching Out
Open Hands
Give It Away to Keep It
Saving Our Own Ass
Twelfth Stepping
Someone Needs Your Help

But Jen put it this way:

Even though the Twelfth Step is working with others, you do service work for you, not them. Service work *helps me.* I really am saving my own ass.

We're told in the Big Book of Alcoholics Anonymous that "if an alcoholic failed to perfect and enlarge his spiritual life through work and self-sacrifice for others, he could not survive the certain trials and low spots ahead" (pp. 14–15). Thus, we appreciate that the Step designed to teach us how to help others is really the Step meant to Save Our Selves.

Through this final Step, we continuously hold fast to the purpose set in our hearts by the previous eleven Steps. We're satisfied with nothing less than living life in full measure and come to realize that living life in full measure is probably our greatest challenge. The Twelfth Step ensures our continuous growth and its simplicity represents *freedom* to us.

> **Step 12: Having had a spiritual awakening as the result of these steps, we tried to carry this message to other chemically addicted persons and to practice these principles in all our affairs.**

Don't Close Your Eyes—It's Time for Your Spiritual Awakening

Spiritual awakening? Now just how does one describe a spiritual awakening? Does this imply a great expectation or a small one? We ask that you don't "expect" anything at all. The spiritual experience can be viewed as a change in consciousness, in whatever form it unfolds for you. Leon explained his experience as "realizing that I didn't need to kill myself to have something better, a better state of mind. Now having a better state of mind, I can have a better state of affairs." That's a spiritual experience? Yep, it sure is. Shelly had a more "burning bush" type of experience:

> I was praying desperately for a sponsor. No one seemed to fit the bill. One day, I walked into an AA club and there sat a woman with twelve years' sobriety, a woman I despised. Elaine seemed pompous and shallow to me. Wanting to glide past her, a force seemed to stop me and a voice ran through my head,

"Ask her to be your sponsor." Hold on a minute, I protested, "I don't even *like* her." I tried to push past but couldn't. "Can we negotiate?" I wailed inwardly. Yet still, I could not move. "Okay," I sighed, and asked her to be my sponsor. *She said, "No!"* "Some joke," I muttered as I strode away. That night Elaine phoned me and said she had had a spiritual experience and God told her, "I am not sending sponsees to you for *them;* I am sending them for you." She asked me if she could be my sponsor! All I can say today is that there couldn't have been a more perfect sponsor for me, and it seems that I had nothing to do with the spiritual experience we both had.

Now that sounds more like a spiritual awakening. Well, maybe so. But there are no set ingredients; you'll get what you need, whether it's a booming voice from the skies, the still small voice from within, or simply a brand-new thought.

Working with Others: Twelfth Stepping

The second part of this Step is what we term Twelfth Step work, "We tried to carry this message to other chemically addicted persons." In early recovery it's not uncommon for us to be evangelistic and impetuously set out to save the world from the ravages of mind-affecting chemicals. We can become so overwrought in our efforts that some members wind up Twelfth Stepping people who don't even have our disease! When the enthusiasm mellows, there are some guidelines and suggestions you may consider following.

Members of AA, NA, and CDA with long-term sobriety teach us to share our experience, strength, and hope. We tell our stories of what it was like, what happened, and what it's like now. After all, we have no other stories or wisdom to convey other than what happened in our own experience. The fellowships also teach us that we're on twenty-four-hour call to anyone who sincerely seeks our help. Remember, people were there when we reached out, and the point at which someone hits bottom and cries out probably won't come during normal banking hours.

The Nine Guidelines for Twelfth Stepping*

1. Stick to your own story. This way you cannot say anything "wrong."
2. Always try to Twelfth Step in groups (three or more), especially late at night.
3. It's best for guys to Twelfth Step guys and girls to Twelfth Step girls.
4. *No* thirteenth stepping! (That's when you decide that the newcomer not only has a drug problem but a sex problem as well and you'll help with that too!)
5. Avoid playing one-upsmanship with new or potential members. (Who used the most of what and how bad a gang you belonged to isn't important.)
6. Don't patronize, preach, condemn, or condone. Simply share.
7. You aren't a professional; an "I don't know" for an answer to a baffling question can keep you genuine.
8. Quietly ask for guidance before beginning.
9. Don't forget the humor, the smile, and the welcoming hug.

When working with others, we remember that we do this as much for ourselves as for them; we Twelfth Step to save ourselves. Nothing brings us back to basics faster than seeing a shattered and shaking sick one going down fast while fighting addiction.

It's not hard to find people to work with. Of course, there will be the newcomers you meet at meetings; and once parents, teachers, and people in authority begin to notice the changes in you, they'll start asking you to talk to other young people in trouble. Also consider listing your name at the local Central Office and submitting your name as a temporary sponsor at the various Internet sites that offer this service.

When any institution solicits our support, we don't turn our backs, even if there are prior resentments or feelings of embarrassment or in-

---

* Guidelines can also be found in the Big Book in chapter 7, "Working with Others," in the NA basic text in chapter 4, "How It Works" (under Step Twelve), and in the CDA text in chapter 11, "Questions: C.D.A. for the Newcomer."

adequacy. We're in a unique position to help potential members in schools, churches, correction centers, and so on. We speak the language of these young people who need help. We know the current slang and can establish a link that's unavailable to older members of our fellowships. We celebrate our youth and recognize its value in working with others. We ask you not to shrink away from this responsibility.

Practicing the Principles: H.O.W.

The third part of the final Step is "to practice these principles in all our affairs." Principles? Each of our Twelve Steps is based on some fundamental ideal or admirable and moral action that we call "principles." Although we may each find different principles in the Steps, here are some common ones:

- honesty
- faith
- courage
- humility
- service
- love
- willingness
- discipline
- perseverance
- consistency
- self-examination
- open-mindedness
- tolerance

The greatest of these are honesty, open-mindedness, and willingness to learn, which have come to be known as the "HOW" of "How to work this program." We're honest, open-minded, and willing to learn in all our affairs. That means with parents as well as with our sponsor, at school as well as at meetings, with cops as well as with members of the fellowship, and with ourselves as well as with friends.

If you don't have a young people's group in your area, there is nothing preventing you from starting a YES group (Youth Enjoying Sobriety). You can begin an AA, NA, or CDA group with the help of older sponsoring members if you feel the need. CDA is always a good choice for young people because their literature, basic text, and meetings encourage you to tell *your whole story* of addiction without censorship. At the same time, CDA encourages members to continue to go to the other support groups for help. Members of this fellowship don't restrict your language (you can be censored in other fellowships, restricted from using drug terminology in one and sobriety terminology in another, making being honest and open in some groups a huge frustration).

Our biggest concern, though, is that you don't insulate yourself by hanging out with only same-age peers, cutting yourself off from the benefit of hard-won experience. A true peer is anyone (from nine to ninety) who's serious about recovery. Of course, identifying with and working with other young people is enjoyable, but becoming a full member of the fellowship(s) is where your true recovery lies. Our disease is the same, our feelings are the same, and most important, our solution is the same. Our common bond is not in the disease, not in the age, not in race, creed, sex, or even in our drug of choice. Our common bond is solely and gratefully in our solution.

JOEY'S STORY

They said, "Joey might have a drug problem." But that was nuts.
How could I have a problem with something I loved so much?

My dad is from Paraguay and my parents divorced when I was ten. Dad moved back to South America and I lived with my mom from then on. My dad visits me, off and on, and we have a pretty decent relationship now, but he's definitely a conservative-type dude. Right after the divorce, I went to school in South America for a year but hated it—I made up stories to get along but was always the odd man out. Mom decided to take me back to the United States, and my dad and sister stayed down there.

I was enrolled in a Catholic school, Saint Ann's, and tried too hard to please people. Kids can automatically detect that phoniness and they single you out. So I went to great lengths to be cool, like smoking cigarettes. Around age twelve, I was at a concert. I met this seventeen-year-old kid there and we were both into music. He wanted to start a band and I lied, as usual, telling him I played the drums, even though I'd only started two weeks earlier. A few days later we met up and he wanted to introduce me to a few of the others who played in the band. I thought, "Sweet!"

"We're going to meet up at Dragon Park," the dude told me and pulled out a bottle of Everclear. "You drink this?" he asked. I said, "Of course," but I'd never had a drink before in my life. This was my first time, so I had to do it right—hard core like I'd seen on TV. The guys mixed a two-liter bottle with soda but it still burned like hell in my mouth. As it passed from hand to hand, my head told me I had to gulp it, not sip it like they were doing. I gulped as much as they let me. When the tingling began, I said, "Awesome!" By the end of the day, they'd lost me and Mom had somehow found me.

I Flat-lined and Loved It

As we drove to the hospital, she kept smacking me to keep me awake. I woke up with tubes down my throat and nose, and a catheter. "Me drinking with seventeen-year-olds! Wow," I thought. I skipped out on my body, no longer just a cursed twelve-year-old, only I had flat-lined and nearly died from alcohol poisoning. Mom wanted to know why. *I didn't know.* All I knew was that *I loved it* and had to learn how to control it and not get caught again.

I began smoking pot. At first there were long intervals between highs, but they soon came closer and closer. Saint Ann's kicked me out for being a little bastard and being the class asshole—Marilyn Manson style. So Mom sent me to an ADD (attention deficit disorder) school where things got worse. When I smoked weed, I was giddy and laughed and felt cool. Acid was even better. I dug the *powerful stuff* that I couldn't control. When I didn't know what would happen, I loved it.

My first drug test at school, I turned up positive and they said, "Joey might have a drug problem." *But that was nuts.* How could I have a problem with something I loved so much? *It wasn't a problem.* Mom fought with me constantly or me with her. She slapped me a few times, demanded money I'd stole, and threatened to send me to military school.

For a short time, I switched to alcohol to pass the drug tests. Finally, some buddies and I got some prescription meds. They did about twelve but I hadn't done any for a while, so I had to move up in the ranks. I took twenty-four. I tried to walk home and everything started changing. My balance was off, a weight was on me, and I couldn't talk. It dried out all the mucus. My body was awake but my mind was asleep. Was I at my childhood house? I kept trying to get into "my old house" but the door was locked. I peeked in the window and "saw" my mom and sister in there and they wouldn't let me in. I was extra pissed and broke in and fell asleep. A few hours later this lady looked down at this kid passed out on her kitchen floor. My eyes were bulging out. In a raspy voice, I talked her into taking me home.

I questioned Mom on why she wouldn't let me in the house. "What are you talking about?" Mom asked. "Go to bed; you need some sleep." That woman came back with the police and my mother was really angry. I ended up back in the hospital. Later at school, I had another drug screening and finally got kicked out—of school, Mom's, everywhere.

They Cut My Long Pink-Dyed Hair

My dad was going to take me but didn't want a pothead for a son and Mom didn't either. So I jetted. I was pretty empty inside and all this shit was happening, but I wouldn't/couldn't consider stopping using. *Drugs were how I coped.* A few people tried to help me. But I just kept expanding on drugs. Mom found me, as usual, and had me sent to a boot camp/wilderness school in Virginia. I had body piercings and long hair and was proud of this. I wanted to be cool, not like that kid I hated, the one my dad liked. That was the kid Dad put in dress clothes and parted his hair to the side, the kid everyone in public school thought was a geek. In the wilderness school, they cut my long pink-dyed hair and took all my piercings.

We had to work cutting timber and hauling our own water and lived in tents. There was seemingly no way to do drugs. But when we went to a supervisor's house to watch a movie, I was into the medicine cabinet first thing and was up to my old tricks. I found Robitussen. I used all my energy to hide my drug taking and it sucked. My body was lean and tan and I looked great on the outside, but on the inside I was a mess.

I would start crying so they wouldn't know I was using. At this program they made everyone "share" their feelings all the time with this psychiatric crap and confronted you if you didn't. I pretended I was lonely and make up a heartthrob about my father not accepting me. I was a chameleon—we all were. The adults were quick at finding out what tricks we used, but we got quicker to earn privileges. It made me proud to earn them, but then drug use superseded that. None of the kids there were happy—even the ones who were five-star kids; they ended up doing the same as me, just playing along to get out.

One guy was my perfect role model, Keenan, a black dude. He was the first black guy I was really close to. I thought he was doing so well. He was court ordered, had been in jail, and had no family. Keenan was doing the program, really doing it, and we got close. I respected him for turning his life around. Keenan was my perfect role model. Later when I had some clean time, I called him to make amends and found out he was dead—a drunk driving crash.

These Older Dudes in AA Sounded Just Like Me!
I felt I was somewhat changing in there like Keenan. For the first time, I consciously felt sorry for the stuff I'd done to the family—but it never occurred to me to *really get sober.* When you were on the substance-abuse-recovery track at camp, you didn't have to share and get confronted all the time, so I joined. I always thought that the AA speakers, those older men, didn't like us kids. But these well-dressed guys came in saying they were *alcoholics.* I didn't believe they were alcoholics, but once they started talking, they sounded just like me! All that crazy stuff we loved to do. I carried their words with me from that time on. So when I was back out using, it really messed with me.

Some things happened when I was there around eight months. A kid got hurt being restrained, a twelve-year-old. He was hospitalized and I was angry at what they did, so I used this for an excuse to run. On a home visit, I stayed awake in my bed until after Mom went to sleep, cut through the screen, and crawled out. At fifteen, I began living on the streets. For a while I lived in the shrubs beside the 7-11, filling water bottles from people's spigots and eating a slice of bread a day. I did insane stuff like meet up with a crazy guy with tattoos all over him. He told me he killed his brother and let me stay at his hotel. I hung with anyone who could get me drugs—I didn't care if they pulled knives, talked crazy, whatever.

I Ended Up in a Gutter Punk House
Eventually I was back in Nashville living in a gutter punk house. One kid's older brother worked and paid the rent—sort of a pseudo-father to the kids. One sixteen-year-old was so burnt up that he looked twenty. I didn't relate to them and drank myself senseless to get "that feeling" but couldn't do anything but drink myself stupid. Those old dudes in

AA had ruined it for me. After three days, I puked on the carpet and couldn't eat or drink. I "knew" I was dying of tuberculosis. Then I heard my mom was in the hospital with a breakdown over my drinking.

Hearing about my mom, I realized I was still causing her pain and AA was screwing with my head. I knew I was powerless, yet continued to drink myself into a stupor. I would run into my old friends and be an asshole. Everything they said got twisted in my head and I scared them off. Everyone was against me in my mind. One day, wallowing alone in the gutter house, I decided *this was it.* I wanted to be sober. I called some friends and they took me to my mom's. She hugged me and slapped me at the same time. Then Mom wanted to put me back into a camp, but I asked her to go to a meeting with me.

Some Think It's a Joke

At the meetings, I was too scared to pick up a white chip. Mom said, "This is fine, but I don't think you know how to be honest, so this won't work for you." She couldn't believe that AA would really work for me. But I kept going. A former student of a sober high school urged me to go there. Coming from the totally structured environment of the wilderness school to this totally unstructured school program was weird, yet I liked it. If you really want recovery, you find the winners in the high school. We students can tell who's serious and who isn't. Some think it's a joke. This new kid says, "Are we *really* supposed to do the Twelve Step thing? Are they *serious?*" and all of us laughed.

In the beginning, I would get different sponsors that were cool like me—my first had tattoos all over. But I wouldn't call and then *blamed them* for my lack of progress! After six months I hit a different bottom, a program bottom. I could see that my best thinking didn't get me very far, so I decided *not to pick* my sponsor. I picked a winner in the program and asked *him* to pick my sponsor for me. He handed me the phone number of a real straight dude, someone I would never have picked, the kind my dad would have approved of. But he was the best! I called him and worked Steps with him. He was someone I could use as a role model, not someone "cool."

Now I'm looking into colleges. Me! I'm content today. I used to sink into the cushions on the couch, bored as hell and wonder where I'd get my next sack of weed. My mom would say, "Why don't you go out and play?" I would answer that it was boring, but I was sitting on the couch bored. Today I go to the park and sit in the sun. It's calm. I'm alone in peace. Not lonely, just peacefully alone.

Hugs and Humor

Speaker's meetings breathe life into my program. I love the sound of happy voices before and after, the hugs, and the humor. Some people bitch about drunkalogs, but humor gets people to identify with them. A good laugh helps—and we're not a boring bunch of guys.

Being lazy is my worse character defect. I sometimes feel over-whelmed and build my own personal little bomb shelter to hide in. Then nothing is accomplished and everything's worse. I need someone to kick my ass and I work a Step to get out of it.

If You Don't Do It, You Don't Get It

If you want recovery, try it our way. You won't be *consumed* any longer and nothing hangs over you like the courts, guilt, and shame. I pray to something—I don't have to call it God; I take yoga and stuff like that. I was born Catholic, so my mental picture of God is with long hair, a beard, and white robe. My new God is not like a father who's going to beat me, whip out the belt, or judge me to be unacceptable. I pray to the universe, admitting that I need help. The simple act of praying helps whether you know Who it goes to or not. It's just the act of doing it. So my advice to you is, "Do it, or you won't ever get it."

CHAPTER 6
Personal Relationships

*"When people made me unhappy, my first inclination was to beat the
hell out of them. The program has taught me to think!"*
—Phil

One of the biggest, all-time excuses we have used for relapse is some
variation of this: "If you had to deal with _____, you'd get loaded
too." More often than not, we fill in the blank with the name of
someone we're in a relationship with, such as a parent, girlfriend or
boyfriend, brother, sister, cop, teacher, or employer. Let's face it—a
hangnail or a thunderstorm is not exactly a big deal. But being on the
verge of expulsion from school, having knock-down-drag-outs with
our folks, wanting to get loaded because we broke up with someone we
loved—these *are serious* and involve the people in our lives, that is, personal relationships.

Don't Pick Up Even If Your Ass Falls Off

Before we go any further, we need to get one thing straight. We do not
pick up because of hassles and pressures in our lives. We pick up because we suffer from chemical dependency. Any other reason we tell
ourselves is only an excuse for doing what we intended to do anyway.
We know that life "problems" don't cause our disease for two very sound
reasons:

1. Everybody has problems, but not everybody is an alcoholic or
   addict.

2. We remember all the times we got high for reasons other than our "problems," like to have fun, to enjoy sex, when we were bored, to fit in, because it was our birthday, because it was Sunday, because it was Monday, because it was any day at all.

Just as our problems don't cause us to drink and do drugs, neither do our personal relationships. We often use relationships as a handy justification for a "slip," but in our hearts we know it was our lack of a sound spiritual program that led to our relapse. Although the pain of a bad relationship is no excuse for using, we do have to face what's going on in our relationships and begin to deal with our feelings. If we don't deal with our feelings, they'll deal with us.

Negative emotions always act like a poison in an addict's system. They cause us to lose touch with our ideals and threaten our conscious contact with our HP. We cannot afford this loss of contact, because it threatens the spiritual foundation upon which our new life is built. Although we're asked to deal with our relationships in Steps Four through Nine, we can also benefit from gaining a greater understanding of our emotions as they relate to recovery. We offer you our observations.

Anger Is One Letter Short of Danger

Anger is probably the most misused emotion of all, causing the most damage to the system. Indeed, we're warned in the Big Book that anger "may be the dubious luxury of normal men" but that it isn't for us (p. 66). Does this mean we can't get angry? Of course not. That would be impossible anyway. Anger is a human emotion. As humans, we will feel it at times, but we simply cannot express it in hurtful and destructive ways. These "R" the four poisons of anger:

- resentment
- retaliation
- revenge
- repression

Nursing anger over long periods of time is what we mean by *resentment*. Resentment is a feeling that causes us to be irrational, grouchy, and casts a shadow over an otherwise sunny sobriety. *Retaliation* is a loss of control (punching someone in the mouth); it causes guilty feelings and a low self-image. Trying to even the score with someone by scheming to make things "fair" is the character defect called *revenge*. In seeking revenge, we decide we're a better manager than God. And finally there's *repression* in which we deny anger, turning it inward, sometimes to the point of causing psychosomatic illness or suicide. All forms of anger have to be dealt with in an honest, open, and healthy way.

Anger is a product of your personal business. Did you know that you're in business for yourself? It's called the Control Business and the sooner you get out of it, the more at peace you'll be with yourself. In all honesty, most of us expect people, places, and things to act according to our will. If they don't, *pow*, we become angry:

- "If only Mom would get off my back and let me go online when she's not home . . ."
- If only Dad would buy me a car . . ."
- If only that department store would drop the charges—I said I was sorry."

When you expect your mom to change the rules, you're trying to control her. When you expect your dad to buy you a car, you want to control what he does with his money. When you want the department store to go easy on you, you want to control how they deal with theft. It's control. It's self-will. It encroaches on the freedom of others. And we make ourselves angry when we don't get our way.

Fortunately, there "R" four ways to deal with anger:

- responsibility (Steps Four and Five)
- remorse (Steps Six and Seven)
- repair (Steps Eight and Nine)
- repeat-*not* (Steps Ten and Eleven)

When Things Go Wrong, Don't Go with Them

If we don't like the way people do things, we should try to do them ourselves; if we don't like how people treat us, we should find friends who suit us better. In the case of parents, we have home rule number one: When under their roof, be under their rule or out in the rain. Because it's so distasteful to be under the control of others, we drop our controls *from* them and amazingly anger is seldom an issue anymore. Dropping controls is as simple as not expecting, demanding, or insisting on getting our own way. When anger is an issue, we pause and think about how we're trying to control the person, place, or thing that triggered our anger and then say something like, "God, I know you didn't really need my help today. I willingly give the controls to You and I will do the next right thing. I trust that the solution to this situation will be in the best interests of all concerned." We remember that God helps those who let Him do His job.

Guilt and Shame

Many people think guilt and shame are the same thing. They aren't. Guilt is a healthy "early warning" emotion. It lets us know when we've done something that doesn't match our values. We might feel pangs of a guilty conscience when we've misled someone, stole money from our mom's purse, or participated in gang violence that hurt, maimed, or even killed others. Guilt is the precursor to Steps Eight and Nine. Guilt is a gift that helps us work our program.

Shame, on the other hand, is when others (including ourselves) try to make us feel "less than" for things we cannot help or for who we are. Others can try to make us feel degraded for being addicts, for things we did while using that cannot be corrected, for our religious beliefs, or they can try to make us feel shamed-filled because we were sexually abused as children.

Shame is a worthless emotion. What good does it do to *feel bad* about mistakes we've made? Or things that can't be undone? Or for who we are? If we feel guilty about something, we simply need to work the action Steps on it, discover the wrong we've done, and right it. Hanging on to guilt and turning it inward into shame will serve no good purpose. God has already forgiven us; when we work our Steps, we forgive ourselves. Anything else is not ours to bear.

FEAR: False Evidence Appearing Real

Fear opens the door for worry, doubt, loneliness, self-pity, *attitude,* and premature gray hair. Some say that fear is the mother of all character defects and we tend to agree. For instance:

- Worry is only a *fear* of tomorrow and the where and when. We solve this by practicing our daily program and living in the here and now.
- Doubt is *fear* of the unknown. It's the fear that maybe God won't give you what you want just the way you want it. Experiencing doubt is a Second and Third Step problem. God either is in charge or He isn't. If you believe your HP is in charge, then you cannot doubt that your HP always has your highest good in mind.
- Loneliness is the *fear* of abandonment. The only reason for loneliness in the fellowship is that you *choose* to be alone. If you use, you use alone; if you die, you die alone; but if you want fellowship and love, here we are.
- Self-pity is the *fear* of not getting our fair share. The thing to remember here is that if we got our fair share of the trouble we've caused, we'd be up to our neck in shit. So we get off the pity-pot, give thanks that we didn't always get what we deserved, and develop an attitude of gratitude.
- "Attitude" is the ultimate form of self-centeredness. It's not necessarily thinking a lot of yourself, but thinking of yourself a lot. It's putting your preferences, ideas, and needs above others and lording these haughtily over them. Like so many other shortcomings, it is also *fear-based.* Having "attitude" is a deep fear of being "less than" and so you act "more than" and drive everyone nuts.

Our purpose in relationships is to cultivate positive emotions like love, patience, tolerance, trust, kindness, and forgiveness. The principle of cause and effect here is simple: if you want love, be loving; if you want forgiveness, forgive; if you want friends, act friendly. The best investment we know of in personal relationships is to "spend self"— give of self, concentrating on what we can do for others and not what they can do for us. When we spend self, the interest from our investment will be tenfold plus.

Our Families

If your immediate family is understanding and supportive of your recovery, consider yourself blessed. If they hesitate or actually disapprove of what you're doing, walk softly. Don't struggle with outdated or clueless attitudes toward your disease. Parents, grandparents, brothers, sisters, aunts, and uncles may not accept you as an alcoholic or addict because of *their* fears, ignorance, and possibly because of drinking and drug problems of their own. Fifteen-year-old Amanda went to live with her dad because of all the trouble she was getting into with drugs. He was supposed to help. She described the experience this way:

> Here's the 411 on my dad: drug addict, alcoholic, drug dealer. So, of course, I lie to him about going to school, steal his drugs, take his money. Then he tells me he doesn't want me living there!

There's no way a parent in this position can help us. Amanda had to go back to live with her mom who did understand addiction—maybe a little too much—because her mom has strict rules about everything, including when and how often Amanda can use the computer. Even though Amanda is clean and sober today, we can hardly blame her mother's caution in giving privileges back to Amanda. What we remember is that "This, too, shall pass." After all, Amanda's mom won't be restricting the use of computers and giving her a curfew when she's twenty. So we tell this to Amanda, as well as to you, "Do the next right thing; this, too, shall pass, and your mom doesn't *owe* you anything!"

Don't expect unrestricted trust from your family members as soon as you get clean and sober. How long did you spend betraying any trust they put in you? Then give them space—some time to come around. They have to *see* you living your new life for a while (and we don't mean two weeks) to be convinced it's not just a fad or phase. Keep in mind, our parents weren't *always* wrong, although it was easier for us to think that than to look at ourselves. Give them a chance to be right occasionally. They may change, surprisingly for the better, the longer you stay clean and sober.

Friendships

When discussing the touchy subject of friendships, there are no rules per se. But listen. It is unwise to hang out with old pals (or new ones) if all you have in common is getting high. Tyron said:

> When I first got sober, I still wanted to hang out with my old friends, so I told them I was an alcoholic and I couldn't drink with them or get high, thinking they'd understand. Well, they thought I was crazy and I was! Staying with dopers, I didn't stay straight very long. The only thing I had in common with them was getting loaded.

Suzi added this:

> If you run with snakes, you're going to get bit. Soon after I got sober, I found a friend who lived near me and I could relate to her, probably because she was into drugs. I started spending a lot of my time with her and her friends. Every time we went out and the pipe was passed around, I would just pass it on, feeling I didn't need to get bothered over some marijuana fumes. One night the pipe came to me and I took it. I got high that night; I got drunk two days later. I got bit.

Not a lot more needs to be said. However, our experience has shown that building sobriety works better without the added burden of fighting doper friends. After all, we're busy fighting the addict who still lives in our head.

Sex

The topic of sex is discussed on page 69 of the book *Alcoholics Anonymous*. You can read our program's very sensible guidelines there. Here are a few additional thoughts on the subject.

Romance and sexual relationships are governed by the same principles as all our other relationships. "Practicing these principles in our affairs" means sex too (pun intended). No matter how we *thought* drugs were enhancing our sexual relationships, throwing up, acting like an ass, and being a show-off appealed only to those who were doing the same thing. Sobriety really did turn out to be the more attractive approach to winning friends and influencing people.

As far as sex goes, there's a saying that we subscribe to, "Sex deepens love and love deepens sex." Physical intimacy transforms everything and playing with it is like playing with fire. This is an area we treat with respect and patience, and we don't play word games to try and justify activities to ourselves. We're especially honest about this area of our lives. Sex is defined as any type of intimacy with the intent of orgasm, whether it is oral, "through the clothes," using the phone, or on the computer. We recognize that *sex is sex*.

A final thought: as powerful a draw as romantic relationships are, they don't come first in our lives. We devote attention to them only after meetings, the program, and Twelve Stepping. Staying clean and sober is ever our priority or there won't be much left of us to have a relationship with.

Put recovery first to make it last!

KITT'S STORY

*She struggled with her sexuality, hating men and the
way they treated her, wondering if she was gay.*

I lived with my grandmother and my mother. My mother worked forty
hours a week and was away a lot, so my grandmother ended up raising
me. I was an only child, pampered and loved by all, but somehow that
wasn't enough for me. By the sixth grade, at least four mothers had
told their children I couldn't play with them, and I was never sure why.
At about that time, I started ditching school with a girl who nobody
cared for. She smoked and had already lost her virginity. We got caught
the second time. The result was that I lost rapport with all the teachers
and cool kids. My grandmother and mother turned on me, it seemed,
and I began talking back. They became suspicious of letting me go out
at night, accusing me of being evil. I remember feeling helpless and
that I was the victim of injustice.

Pay a Dollar, Buy a Pill, and Swallow It

Between the seventh and eighth grades, an interesting development took
place. I began to hear talk about a drug called LSD. I saw "ACID" carved
on the back stairs and bathrooms at school. I started hearing words like
flower child, groovy, hippy, love, peace, free, and *psychedelic.* Terribly curi-
ous and awed, a friend and I decided to go to a park because we had
heard that a bunch of hippies were there. We sat in a group, smoked
joint after joint, and drank wine, waiting to see what happened. I
wanted to be cool. Someone said to me, "Pay a dollar, buy a pill, and
swallow it." Finally I did. After a while, I began to feel the effects. The
whole world was churning, buzzing, and moving. Feelings, thoughts,
cars, people were coming at me fast and all at the same time. I passed
the night at a girlfriend's—my first night of sneaking away from home.
Finally the effects of the drug wore off, and I went home. I felt so

distant from my family. I wanted to feel warm and loved, but that morning those things were impossible.

Wherever You Go, There You Are

Situations at home reached a no-win point. It had become a cold war. Each of us was hurt, sick, and tired. My mother decided we'd move to our own apartment, away from my grandmother, "so our troubles would be over." Yeah, my mother would let me be free! I had little idea of what she was going through and wasn't interested enough to find out. I wanted her to smoke pot and be a different person. I wanted her to understand about all the groovy things that were going on and all the groovy people I met. Most of those people, incidentally, were men whose prime interest was taking me to bed. When I wasn't in school, I was running around with an assortment of guys, getting terribly drunk or stoned. As months went by, I took LSD quite a bit by myself and began to wander aimlessly around town. Other kids looked down at me and thought I was weird. I strayed around, trying to belong, but nobody was terribly responsive.

That year I accidentally overdosed on Seconal. Everyone thought it was a suicide attempt, and that convinced me that no one did understand. They thought I was screwed up, while I thought I was as right as Jesus. Life became a nightmare. Among other things, I was suspended from school, went to jail, and was raped by a guy I was partying with. It was awful.

All I could think about was getting high. I copped some acid and after school called my mother at work and told her I wouldn't be home. I went downtown. Some people picked me up, and not knowing what was wrong, they called the police, who took me to the psych ward. Because I didn't come down, I was transferred to a private mental hospital. That lasted five months, and I continually used drugs and alcohol throughout my stay. Because of my continued drug use, they couldn't really help me, and when I got out, I felt more estranged from people.

Nothing Changes, If Nothing Changes

After running away, getting more loaded and spaced out, I went back home. I stayed high and drunk through the summer. At the end of summer my mother abandoned me, moving to Maryland, and I don't remember saying good-bye to her. Now I was a ward of the court and was sent to the state hospital. I weighed ninety-five pounds, was anemic and completely irrational. Once more, I was in a mental institution, again five months. I got kicked out for confessing to setting a fire that I had known nothing about. On departure, I felt more helpless and hopeless. My only solution was to stay loaded.

I went from there to a girl's home. I got into needles and managed to keep myself stoned out. But I broke all the rules at their house and again was kicked out. I went to a foster home, and, while there, I went to jail several times for being drunk and disorderly. My tolerance for alcohol had gone down and I blacked out every time I drank.

When I turned eighteen, I drank champagne on my emancipation day and I was *free,* or so I thought. I started running with some women junkies, clinging to them, having sex with some of the women heroin addicts, seeking the affection and the tenderness that wasn't to be found in our larger world. I started turning tricks for money, for booze, and for drugs. In the next years, I got beat up, busted, hitchhiked across the country alone, got pregnant, aborted, got raped, and, several times, detoxed. During those days, I went to bed with a lot of people, just wanting to buy some time with them, hating the loneliness. I struggled with my sexuality, hating men and the way they treated me, wondering if I was gay. I was anything but free.

You Have to Work a Full Program in a Halfway House

At age twenty-one, after many a quart, fix, and pill, I ran into a woman I had met at an AA meeting. She took me to another meeting where they talked about my life being unmanageable and my powerlessness over alcohol. I don't know how much I understood, but I knew for the first time in my life that I sincerely wanted to quit drinking.

The next day, I went to an AA club. I sat and talked to different people, and one of them suggested I go to a halfway house. I did just what they said because I had no fight left in me. The woman who had taken me to the first meeting came and gave me a book. She told me to take very good care of myself, saying that I had a disease like diabetes. She told me not to worry about anything and to stay away from situations that upset me. She talked about her drinking, how sick she had been, and what the Twelve Steps had done for her.

Do Ninety in Ninety

I'm not sure how or why, but I went to ninety meetings in ninety days and I started to work the Steps of Alcoholics Anonymous. I was confused and full of fear sometimes. I prayed to a God I wasn't sure existed. At meetings, I said that I was an alcoholic, even though I wasn't sure of that. But something happened that had never happened before. My ears were half open and what all these people were telling me made sense. I began to look forward to meetings.

After several months, I was encouraged to get an apartment, and so I moved out of the halfway house. My apartment manager was in AA; people from AA helped me with food, cigarettes, and money until I could get a job. They gave me phone numbers and told me to call anytime. Somehow, over the months, the program of Alcoholics Anonymous began to sink in. I started learning and growing. A lot of my fears fell away.

Slowly, meeting after meeting, I learned about my illness. I learned about resentment and fear, although a lot of what was said at meetings confused me. I struggled with the Steps, talking to people, trying to understand what they meant. Listening to people sometimes when I didn't want to, I found out that I wasn't like people who weren't addicted. I didn't function the way they did. I struggled with problems like jobs, people, my sexuality, Christianity, and my identity. And for every question, fellow addicts had an answer.

"We will comprehend the word serenity. . . ." (pp. 83–84, Big Book)

Eventually I found gay AA meetings, and slowly I'm learning how to find my real feelings. I learned to live one day at a time. I learned how to accept myself as an alcoholic and a human being. I learned about my own self-deception and the ways my mind twists the truth. I searched for God, finding it within me. Slowly I became acquainted with a feeling that I had never felt before—serenity.

I now experience many things that I had missed for years, and hear and read things that enable me to deal with life on its own terms. Tolerance for me and for others is something I am learning, and surprisingly, I'm learning to love myself. I have found Narcotics Anonymous where I am beginning to learn about drugs from a new standpoint. There's much more for me to learn about all these things. But I feel that a door has been opened. Through God and the fellowship of AA, I've found a new life. And most significantly, I've found that I never *have* to drink or take drugs again.

CHAPTER 7

To Parents, by Parents

"I didn't cause it, I can't cure it, and I can't control it. These are the three Cs of Families Anonymous, precious points to remember when dealing with those who suffer from this disease of addiction."
—Kathy H.

You may be shocked when you first learn that your child is or may be an alcoholic and drug addict. Generally, parents don't fully realize that their child is in real trouble with drugs and alcohol until something *terrible* happens, like an accident, expulsion from school, arrest for criminal activity, attempted suicide, or overdose. Yet clear signs are usually present long before the incident happens, and probably someone tried to tell us, but parents have difficulty believing this kind of trouble knocks at their door—*"not my kid!"* When their child begins to experience real trouble in school, with friends, and in the family, parents tell themselves:

• Boys will be boys.
• I did the same things.
• Let them have fun while they're young.
• Everyone gets caught once in a while.
• What do you expect? She or he is only a teenager.

Most parents don't know their children need help until it's too late. So here you are, reading this book when everything has spun so out of control; you're not sure how you can ever right it again.

And we're going to ask you *not to right it,* which may further shock you until the full nature of the addictive diseases and recovery becomes clear. That's why we wrote this chapter, to give you the benefit and strength of our experience so you can make clear, sound decisions about what you want to do and what will or will not help the situation with your son or daughter.

You Didn't Cause It

As parents, we can't help but be dismayed because we honestly believed our child could never become seriously involved with drugs or alcohol—or if he or she did, we as a family could handle anything. But you've probably already admitted that nothing is working to solve this problem: your parenting, your family unit, and other tried-and-true family resources. You may be scared, certainly feeling guilty, furious at your child, even angrier with "experts" and other "authorities" who don't seem to be helping. Most of all, you wonder, "What did I do wrong?" Kathy H., who contributed to this chapter, relates:

> I helplessly watched him spiral out of control. He became a stranger—a liar and a thief. He wasn't going to school and he wasn't coming home. He was staying on the streets with the local homeless, sleeping in cars, and panhandling. I searched the Internet for answers but couldn't afford the wonderful-looking schools I found online. I took him to a psychologist I trusted, who reluctantly told me that my son was mentally ill and headed for disaster. I had absolutely no control over his behavior and I was scared to death. I felt like the ultimate failure as a parent.

You haven't failed your child, and likewise your child hasn't failed you. Addiction is a *disease* and just as you wouldn't have "failed" your child if he or she suffers from juvenile diabetes, you haven't failed your child because his or her brain chemistry isn't functioning properly. This is the time to read the first part of chapter 1, which explains the nature of this disease. The sooner you let yourself off the hook, the faster you can get to the heart of the problem and help with the solution.

What really matters today is your child's sobriety and your sanity. This disease is *not a reflection on you as a parent*. If neighbors, other family members, or the school system blame you with "Do something about that incorrigible kid of yours" or if they imply that better parenting could have prevented the problem, or some such recrimination, explain as gently as possible what you're learning about addiction, what you're doing about your child's addiction, and refuse to accept any blame. A father explains his viewpoint:

> I don't accept the "fact" that I or my child am to blame. We are all victims of circumstances and do the best we can to cope with the "injustices" of life. There is good in everything if we look for it. I believe my child has gained great strength of character as well as great insight into himself and life because of these experiences. What a beautiful happening.

It's difficult to escape this notion that you are at fault. Even child development experts blame parents when children have problems. Yet, you won't get far in the solution until you leave this destructive notion behind. Phyllis and David York, founders of ToughLove, explain in their book *ToughLove:*

> The way in which we therapists blame is by thinking and acting as if the children in the family are victims of their parents' anomalies. As long as parents are accepting the rap for their offsprings' behavior their children can't change. (p. 67)

You Can't Control It
We all try and eventually come to terms with the fact that we aren't going to control this disease. When we learn that we didn't cause it, we

had to let go of the guilt. And as we learn we can't control it, we have to deal with anger, rage, and intense frustration. Kathy H. in Families Anonymous told another parent this:

> Of course you're mad at him! His using has turned your life upside down! Addicts are self-absorbed, unthinking train wrecks! But when you stop being angry and start feeling guilty about the anger, [grin] remember that it's probably the disease you are angry about. The disease hijacked the brain of that beautiful boy and turned him into a stranger. Yes, it was his choice to start using and it probably doesn't matter much right now as to why he made that decision. The horror of addiction is that after a while, the brain chemicals are altered and free will goes out the window.

Yet, it's difficult to let go of the belief that we can somehow control, if not the disease, at least our child. Through your son's or daughter's addiction you will know deep feelings of powerlessness and helplessness. Addiction isn't a skinned knee that we can put a bandage on or some flu that a bit of chicken noodle soup and some crayons and a coloring book will sooth away. Trying to "fix" addiction, we slam into one wall after another after another until it brings us to our knees. CeeCee explained it this way:

> I, too, wanted to learn *all* I could about his addiction. I knew what he might do, what he would do, what he "for sure" was going to do, and what he could do to recover. When he entered rehab, I was present at all the family sessions, listening and learning. I went to Web sites (Crackbusters.com comes to mind) and printed out page after page of things that might help him. I educated myself to the point that if they gave diplomas, I would have gotten a master's. I would be prepared to "lead" him through his recovery, to be there every Step of the way with him. And what happened? He relapsed twice after rehab.

He never read any of the many printouts I worked so hard to compile for him. He wouldn't even talk to me about it.

People who are already in Twelve Step programs—whether it be AA or Al-Anon, Families Anonymous, or another program—have a basic understanding that the young person has to *want help* and has to be motivated from within; we can't do it for them. Sometimes we must take a lot of beatings before we give up the delusion that we can somehow fix this. We may very well understand it in our head; our hearts don't agree so easily. Kathy H. continues:

Powerless? Me? No way—I am Mom, hear me roar, and you just watch me protect my baby and fix these problems. After all, it's my job to take care of my son any and every way I know how. I will go to any lengths to find a solution for his problems. But wait. They're *his* problems someone said. Yeah? So? I've been solving his problems all his life and he's a minor and it's not his fault because there is a genetic disposition to alcoholism in the family.

Often the very things we do to help our child are what makes it so very easy for him or her to keep using. This is called "enabling." When we enable, we're essentially not allowing our alcoholic/addict to experience the consequences of his or her own actions. When we enable, we *feel as if* we're doing the loving thing, nurturing and helping our child through the rough spots of adolescence. But we may actually be doing the very things that allow the disease to win. Wadetta W. puts it this way:

I had finally come to the realization that every time I took him in, fed him, gave him things, I was actually doing the same as buying his drugs. I have taken him back off and on over the years. Finally, I was able to sit with him in the car tell him how very much I loved him, and put into words my feelings about what I was doing "for" him. I was, in essence, purchasing the drugs that would ultimately kill him. I loved him too much to contribute to his suicide. I owed it to God to not be contributing to the death of one of His children. It was bittersweet and I cried all the way home, sat on pins and needles till I would get word from him, etc. Even with him in prison, I start getting the old grip in the gut when he is not able to call or write.

You Can't Cure It

You've dealt with the guilt, you've faced the anger and helplessness, and now you must work on surrender. This means giving up the ghost on you doing it, handling it within the family, and/or solving the problem "your" way. You must now look to people who have successfully dealt with addiction and their own children. You have two main areas to work on: you and your kid.

Help for You First

First you. We want you to seek information and support for yourself first. If your child had leukemia, you'd learn as much as possible about the disease in order to help your child survive, right? Alcoholism and other addictions, unattended, can be as fatal as any cancer. Not just any professional will do either. If you sought help for a child with cancer, you wouldn't go to a podiatrist, would you? You would seek out an oncologist. So we ask you not to go to experts or support groups unless they *specialize in addiction*. This is very important. In fact, you may be able to get the help and education you seek from a community support group. Here's what we recommend:

1. **Al-Anon Family Groups.** A fellowship for men, women, children, and adult children whose lives have been affected by the compulsive drinking of a family member or friend. This group has the most in-person meetings and you're likely to find a local group for support.
   Write: Al-Anon Family Groups, Inc., 1600 Corporate Landing Parkway, Virginia Beach, VA 23454-5617

Call: (757) 563-1600 or (888) 4AL-ANON

Online contact: WSO@al-anon.org or
http://www.al-anon.alateen.org

2. **Co-Dependents Anonymous.** A Twelve Step self-help program of recovery from codependency, where each of us may share our experience, strength, and hope in our efforts to find freedom and peace in our relationships with ourselves and others.

Write: CoDA, P.O. Box 33577, Phoenix, AZ 85067-3577

Call: (706) 648-6868

Online contact: coda.usa.nsc.outreach@usa.net or
http://www.codependents.org

3. **Families Anonymous.** A Twelve Step fellowship for relatives and friends concerned about the use of drugs, alcohol, or behavioral problems. This particular fellowship seems to focus on parents of addicted children.

Write: Families Anonymous, P.O. Box 3475, Culver City, CA 90231-3475

Call: (800) 736-9805

Online contact: famanon@FamiliesAnonymous.org or
http://www.FamiliesAnonymous.org

4. **Nar-Anon.** A worldwide organization offering self-help recovery to families and friends of addicts. A Twelve Step program structured like Al-Anon. Provides group packet for starting new groups.

Write: Nar-Anon, 302 West Fifth Street, Suite 301, San Pedro, CA 90731

Call: (310) 547-5800

5. **ToughLove.** A self-help program for parents, kids, and communities dealing with the out-of-control behavior of an adolescent. Parental support groups help parents take a firm stand so that kids learn to take responsibility for their behavior.

Write: ToughLove, P.O. Box 1069, Doylestown, PA, 18901

Call: (800) 333-1069 or (215) 348-7090 (day)

Online contact: http://toughlove.org

It may also be very helpful to attend open AA, NA, and CDA meetings as well as your personal support group. Be sure you attend an "open" meeting meant for all interested parties as opposed to a "closed" meeting intended only for those in recovery. "Open" or "closed" should be noted on any meeting list you use; you can also call the contact person and verify before you attend. Listen at these meetings; they'll tell you how to work on *your problems* first. Many of us have balked at this. "It's their problem, not mine," we wail. It's their *responsibility* to get well, but a problem that affects the entire family. And when you try to control the uncontrollable, then it becomes your problem also.

Help for Your Child

If you've recognized that addiction is a major problem before a terrible event has occurred, you must encourage your child to seek help from his or her peers in AA, NA, and CDA groups. Take him or her to a Twelve Step club and ask for someone willing to talk to a newcomer;* try to locate a young people's meetings, and bribe your kid into attending a few; call your closest Twelve Step service office and ask for some good speakers meetings and go as a family. Find professional help and *pressure your child to accept it* or to attend treatment if you have the means. Expose him or her to whatever resources you find in your community but realize that your initial attempts will probably illicit only scorn. Remember, adolescents don't usually seek help on their own. First, they need to be exposed to recovery to know it's possible. Second, they need to face the consequences of their using behavior to

---

*A Twelve Step club is usually a private endeavor where interested parties open a room or building to people interested in recovery. These clubs house meetings, often have coffee and snacks available, sometimes contain gift shops and halls for dances or large meetings, and usually remain open so that clean and sober people have a safe place to hang out when they aren't at meetings. They can be found in the phone book under "alcoholism" and are often named "Alano Club." You can also call any treatment center and its employees should be able to locate the club closest to you.

be motivated. Your job is to make their exposure to recovery possible and then *stop enabling* in order to kick-start some incentive within.

When we say expose your child to his or her peers in the programs, we're not talking about age-mates but rather peers in recovery. Your child's peers in recovery can be same-age friends or senior citizens; the common bond is the solution they've found together. Often a parent seeks support that is *only* from professionals who treat the young person exclusively with other young people. Some parents and professionals are afraid of exposing kids to adults with more "serious problems," thinking they might be a bad influence or pose a predatory-type threat to them.

However, the disease is the *real* threat, not people in recovery. You cannot shield your child from exposure to predatory people. They're found in our neighborhoods, in the church, in the legal system, in the schools, and in the Boy Scouts and Girl Scouts. It would be foolish to say your child will not find these types of people in Twelve Step programs. They will be there. So you must rely on the same protection in the fellowships as you do now with other organizations. This is to warn your adolescent strongly, teach him or her assertive skills, and explain what to watch out for.

Sometimes we resent that others are able to reach our child when we were not. It can be very difficult to face that we're no longer the "fixer." Donald explains:

> It was at this point [his son's beginning recovery] that as a parent, I found it most painful. This was mainly because experience told me that I could not be the one to help and advise. AA and NA would work for him, if I stayed out of it. For me to selfishly impose my role as father or close friend [which he and I became in this struggle] would have complicated things for him. Now, he needed to keep it simple.

The folks in these programs are your child's lifeline and it's best not to interfere in the strong bonds your child will form with his or her sponsor and fellow travelers on Recovery Road. This doesn't mean, however, that you allow your child to date inappropriate people, abuse curfews, or generally have all the rights of adulthood while still a minor and under your care. Boundaries are important to maintain. Allowing your child to find his or her own recovery doesn't mean he or she gets to selfishly and irresponsibly do what he or she wants. In fact, the Twelve Step programs will be telling your child precisely that he or she *must be* responsible to and for himself or herself and must not be self-centered. So, actually, you will find the Twelve Steps and the fellowships to be your greatest ally as a parent and in supporting family values.

Professionals and Treatment

Ideally, the situations described above, where you send your child to community-based self-help programs and groups, are preferable to other forms of treatment. However, we know that most young people don't voluntarily seek help for addiction. Most of the time they have to be forced by parents, the legal system, or other professionals in the school system and mental health field. When seeking professional help, here are a few guidelines:

1. The most expensive treatment is not necessarily the best. Research your community, browse online, and ask in your support group for resources that will match your situation exactly. Sometimes the no- or low-cost forms of treatment are as good, or better, than their more expensive counterparts.
2. Multigenerational treatment has the best outcome rates for every-body.* While there are some very well-planned adolescent-only centers, consider that any long-term recovery is going to be in the real world. If state laws allow it, try placement first in a multi-generational center. If state laws don't allow it, try to locate a cen-ter that integrates the young person in community self-help and combines groups and lectures with older clients.

*Shelly Marshall, "The Multigenerational Treatment Setting for the Chemically Dependent Adolescent: Impact on Cost, Quality, and Treatment Outcomes," *The Journal of Addictive Diseases* 18, no. 4 (1999).

3. Don't let other people's prejudices get in the way of sound decisions. You know your child and family background best. If you're a scientologist, their drug program Nar-conon might work best for you. If you're a Christian, you might want to look at Overcomers Outreach or Teen Challenge for answers. Some people quake in their boots at the thought of a boot-camp treatment facility, yet we know many young people have greatly benefited from the discipline. What we're saying is that one size does not fit all. Arm yourself with the facts, and then do what's best for your family.

4. Shy away from any program that identifies you as the problem and source of your child's addiction. If a professional implies that your learning how to communicate with your child will somehow manage his or her addiction or that better parenting skills might have prevented the addiction, you're in the wrong place. Addiction is a disease. Although you want to learn all you can to be a part of the solution and not a part of the problem, dealing with your issues is going to make you a better person, not cure your child's addiction.

5. Post-treatment. Do not send your child back to the same school if there isn't a Twelve Step or sobriety group right at the educational institution. Recovery doesn't work if an addict is dumped right back with his or her drug crowd. Consider a GED or community college where there are meetings on campus, a sober high school, homeschooling, or sending your child away to relatives who have access to a sober school environment. This is sometimes more difficult than finding good treatment, but if not heeded, can destroy all your progress. Jane M. shared her experience:

My son entered an outdoor therapy program at the age of fifteen, and I had a huge sense of relief that upon his return, our lives would return to normal. Absolutely nothing could have been further from the truth. My sense of denial was in high gear for months as I watched his old behaviors resurface when he returned to his former public high school.

Jane's son, now twenty, is clean, sober, and successful. This she attributes to his eventual admission into a Tennessee Sober High School based on the Twelve Step model. These schools are few and far between, but they can be found.

Meeting Makers Make It

After treatment, continue to support your son's or daughter's attendance in a self-help fellowship. Treat the meetings like medicine. Never restrict meetings or withhold Twelve Step activities as a punishment to express your anger. Keep the following in mind:

1. Meetings aren't for fun; they're serious therapy. We wouldn't stop a sick child from seeing a physician as a means of punishment.
2. We add to the resentment and animosity by preventing him or her from talking to maybe the only people who really understand. Our child is not playing an attention game; alcoholism is a serious disease.

Emily has to fight her mother's attitudes as well as her own cravings and temptations. She explained:

Parents don't understand how hard it is. My mom thinks I'm trying to get sympathy or make excuses. If you're going to stay sober, you have to go to meetings. My mom needs to lighten up.

And Brittany had a similar problem:

Mom told me to walk to meetings. I wanted to tell her to go to hell. Why doesn't she give me a second chance? I wish my mom knew what it was like to be an addict.

Letting Go and Letting God

When nothing you do works, when you discover that all your help and picking up the pieces is simply allowing your child to stay in denial and disease, when you realize that paying his or her bills is the same as buying him or her drugs, it's time to let your son or daughter go. Allow your child to face the consequences of his or her own actions. At times, this may mean painfully letting him or her go to jail or be expelled from school. But it will pay off in the long run in life experience for your kid. *Do not do for them what they can do for themselves.* Growing up after forty will be more difficult for both of you. None of us wants to see our kids reach senility before reaching maturity! A husband and wife expressed their experience of letting go like this:

> I just had a talk with my husband about my worst fear that our son could be dead and we would wish we had intervened in some way. He reminded me that we have intervened many, many times before and it would only help for a little while. Our son has lied to us many times about putting his drug life behind him, changing his ways, and listening to us. My husband feels that it is up to our son now. My head knows this is right, but my heart says, "This is a child who is up against a terrible enemy." I know God is greater. I look forward to a day when I can stop saying I am "trying" to let go of it and have the peace that comes from truly doing so.

Not all of our children live. Losing them in death is our greatest fear and it's a tough balancing act trying to do the right thing. Another mother, who wanted to remain anonymous, shared some heartbreaking news when she told her FA (Families Anonymous) group that she couldn't give advice to "let go." She said she did let go and "now my daughter is dead." While drinking and driving, this girl had a terrible accident the day after her twenty-second birthday. This heartbroken mother will always wonder if her intervention could have made a difference. She also told her group just two weeks after the death of her girl, "Make sure your child always knows you love her. When there is nobody else, Mom and Dad are there." There are no shortcuts, just faith. Cinda says:

I don't think there are any shortcuts to letting go. We all have to try to do things on our own until *we* decide we need to let go . . . just like the addict. . . . Only *they* can decide when enough is enough. I often look at my panicky feelings that relate to my son as my addiction flaring up. For so many years, he was my drug of choice.

You have two things you must do now: *don't enable* and *let your child know you love him or her no matter what.* The second is usually the easy part; it's the first that's the bugaboo of all parents with addicted children. You'll be hearing lots of terms about being an enabler and codependent to your child's disease. Remember when you were expecting your first child? Everyone became an expert on how to have a baby, feed it, bathe it, raise it, and all of these people were telling you what to do, *their way.* Lots of folks will be telling you now how to deal with this disease (if they even believe it's an illness) and giving you advice about what to do and not do with your child. Although we implore you to educate yourself, join a support group, seek professional help if you need it, *don't let others make your decisions.* You are the one who has to live with them and thus you must be the one to make them.

And finally, never confuse your love for your child with your hatred of the disease. Loneliness is a fear we all share. Let your child know he or she is not alone, that you will be there, always. No matter what, there's a light waiting for your son or daughter when he or she wants to come home—clean and sober that is! And as your child's recovery begins, you may find that you even enjoy sharing this great adventure with him or her.

CINDA'S STORY

This is the last *time I'm going to give you money. . . .* Do you hear me????" *Always I got,* "Mom, this is the last time!" *It never was.*

My name is Cinda and my youngest son has been addicted to drugs since he was sixteen. For the first six years of his addiction I lived in *hell* twenty-four hours a day. I'd like to tell you what changed in my life.

The way I found out my son was an addict was when he stayed out all night one Saturday and came home without his car. He had sold it for drugs. The same car his grandfather had just bought him for $3,000. I bought back his car for $900, and I immediately sent him to an inpatient rehab. Before the first bill came for the rehab facility, he was out using again.

He Needed Money so His Dealers Wouldn't Hurt Him

For the next five years I begged, bribed, threatened, and forced him into three other rehab facilities, only to find he began to use again briefly after getting out. Eventually it had become routine for him to call me in the wee hours of the morning to bring him money so his dealers wouldn't hurt him. Each time I would jump in the car and race to his rescue. With each rescue I said, "This is the *last* time I'm going to give you money. . . . *Do you hear me????*" Always I got, "Mom, this is the *last time!*" It never was.

One morning after returning from a 3:00 A.M. rescue trip, I sat in the dark living room and told God that I had had enough. I no longer wanted to wake up in the morning. Life was too painful to bear another day. I begged God to let me go in my sleep. In my heart I knew all my attempts at rescuing my son were the same as loving him to death, but I just couldn't stop. I actually thought my death might even save him.

How Could Me Working a Program Help My Son?

I had heard about people getting on chat lines on the Internet, so I got on my computer and started searching . . . praying I would find some-one to help me. I did a search on cocaine and found the online Co-Anon group. I read their home page and thought, "What the heck, I'll subscribe. . . . What do I have to lose?" I slept for a couple of hours, and before I went to work, I logged on and checked my e-mail. There were five parents who greeted me and briefly told me their story.

Immediately I felt this blanket of comfort drift down over me. These people understood what I was going through! I joined the group with the hope of finding a way to save my son, and I sadly found out I don't have that power. At first I was depressed, but I couldn't tear my-self away from the group. For the first time since my son's addiction, I had found people who truly understood the pain I was living with. Suddenly I needed these people like I needed oxygen. I was online with the group eight-plus times a day. During the first three months I heard all about "working the program" and had *no idea* what that meant and truly didn't see how it was going to help my son, but I kept reading.

I Was Screaming at God to Save My Son

During this time, my son was getting worse and worse. I was still res-cuing him and I was still in great pain. As I heard the other members share how they were working their program and finding comfort, I fi-nally decided to give the program a try. I started focusing on the Steps. I even got to the point where I was comfortable taking the phone off the hook at night, and finally I was getting a good night's sleep. One thing I lacked was a relationship with God. I spent every waking hour praying, begging, screaming at God to save my son, and things just kept getting worse.

Then, one night I forgot to take the phone off the hook, and sure enough he called in a panic for money or he'd be hurt. I leapt out of bed and headed for the car. As I was driving around looking for an ATM machine, I was praying (screaming and crying) to God, "God, give me the strength to do what is best for my son and myself." When

I reached our appointed meeting place, he got in the car and we held each other crying. Suddenly I heard this voice say, "I love you unconditionally, but I have no money for you." I was in total shock. This was the first moment that I realized I hadn't stopped at an ATM machine for money. I left thinking that that might be the last time I was going to see my son, but I had turned him over to God. I let him go. Within a week my son began his first year of not using since he was sixteen years old. He was twenty-two at the time.

I'm not sure that an action on my part promoted God to "do" something for my son, but I do know that up until that moment I had never felt such comfort. I was trusting a Power greater than myself to look after my son. This didn't mean I expected this Power to protect my son from pain or even death, but I did trust this Power to know what was best for both of us, and I was giving this Power the room to work.

I don't "expect" God to give me what I want; I "expect" God to give me what I need. And I continually pray for the strength to accept His will in my life as well as my son's.

CHAPTER 8
Are They All Out to Get Us?

*"Most people are busy enough not to have to go out looking for trouble;
it's usually dropped in their lap."*
—Paul

Many an addicted adolescent has committed a crime, been prosecuted, classified a delinquent, and thrown into some correction center, all the while not understanding what happened. They certainly never intended to be locked away. Many more young people who are chemically dependent, through constant "troublemaking," have been labeled "incorrigible," again locked away, and treated for behavioral problems. Very often, *more often than not,* the loss of freedom does not result from some innate criminality, but from a progressive and incurable disease.

It's understandable that the symptoms of our disease would baffle parents, authorities, even us. Look at the multitude of situations from sticky to tragic we get into:

- shoplifting
- burglary
- running away from home
- sexual offenses
- pregnancy
- dope dealing
- expulsion from school
- gang activity
- drive-by shootings

- car wrecks
- loitering
- prostitution

These only scratch the surface of what "troublemaking" we are capable. Although we believe that being committed to institutions for behavioral problems isn't the solution to anybody's addiction, we must hold ourselves strictly accountable for any damages caused through our disease. If we've broken the law, we must accept the consequences of the legal system. Nevertheless, we understand that the solution doesn't lie in punishment, but principle—the principles we learn to live by in our new life. We learn to accept that the "punishment" of confinement is a debt we owe to society and that living by Twelve Step "principles" is the debt we owe to ourselves.

It wasn't so long ago that law enforcement simply incarcerated young addicts. They did their time, took their punishment, and remained as confused as everyone else, thinking they were "born bad, branded, and a real e-tard." Today, society generally accepts that no amount of correction or punishment is going to help until the underlying issue is addressed: chemical dependency. And thankfully, many courts now sentence addicted criminals to treatment rather than prison—or at least they incorporate some addiction treatment into the correction facility package.

Recover or Recaught?
We have much to be grateful for when considering law enforcement officials and drug courts. Young people seldom seek help voluntarily. So rarely does a person under twenty seek help on his or her own that the program has a saying: *Young people don't get sober; they get caught.*

"When an old man told me that in a meeting, it made me real angry," said Bethany, "to be disrespected like that." The answer to that is, "Yeah, but I'm not going to get recaught; I choose to recover."

We don't care if the courts sent you, if your parents demanded it, or a school counselor did. All we care about is that you're here and getting help. Getting help is the point. Don't make a point of overreacting every time someone mentions your youth. Some younger members stay on high alert looking for things to upset them. It doesn't matter what an older member says, from "You're too young to be an alcoholic" to "You're lucky to find the program at such a young age." They use any excuse to find fault with others and distance themselves. If someone at a meeting says some ignorant thing, cut that person some slack. Spencer put it this way:

> My respect has to be earned. I'm not just another b.s. teenager here just to get my slip signed. They'll see as I grow and stay sober.

Ask yourself, "Am I just another b.s. teenager getting my slip signed? Will I just go play the game, go out, and get recaught? Or will I choose to recover?"

Our Choices Determine Our Consequences

We ask parents and young people not to assume that the authorities are wrong for demanding that we be legally accountable for our actions. Many lives have been saved by the grace of the judicial system in forcing young adults to face what they've done and what their addiction took away from them. One mother, Cinda (whose story appears in chapter 7), observed:

> My son has been to jail a couple of times. . . . The longest time was two nights. I never bailed him out and I told him I never would. The way I see it is, if he did the crime, he needs to pay his dues. My ex-boss was a retired warden of our state prison. One thing that always stuck with me was the stories he'd tell me of how so many people turn their lives around in jail. I'm a teacher at our community college and university, and one semester I had a student who was on parole. He came up to me after class to tell me his parole officer was going to be checking

in from time to time to make sure he was attending class. Then he proceeded to tell me, with tears in his eyes, that going to prison was the best thing that ever happened to him. He said nothing else would ever have been able to turn his life around except that experience. From that moment on, I have felt that if my son did something that caused him to go to jail, it may just be exactly what God intended to have happen, and I may be causing harm if I meddled.

If the legal system *doesn't* make adolescents responsible, it often helps out if the parent does.

Wadetta W. makes this clear:

When I had to file charges of unlawful use of a vehicle, see my son crying in the police car while begging me that he didn't want to go to prison, all I could tell him was that I loved him and God loved him and neither of us would abandon him. He knew he did wrong and he knew what the consequences would be. I was with him at most of his court appearances, hard as it was. I followed through and am not sorry that I let him suffer the consequences of his actions.

When we seemingly "get away with it," we have no real reason to quit using. If the ramifications of our out-of-control behavior don't hit home, then sooner or later we're back where we began. Mike describes what happened to him when his father got him off of some serious charges. A patrol car had spotted Mike, his girlfriend, and some friends drive up a deserted road in the hills, turn out the lights of their vehicles, and light up some joints. When it was just long enough for them to get good and high, the cops busted them. Mike escaped (abandoning his girlfriend) and ran through the brush, tearing his clothes, ripping his feet to shreds, and spending the night totally paranoid, using the brambles and weeds for camouflage. He recalls:

Morning came slowly, but finally it was light. I tried to stand up on feet that were swollen and sore. I was able to start walking by taking each painful step a little at a time. Now that I was thinking straight, I realized the only rational course of action was to go home. My father was a policeman. Because I agreed to cooperate with the authorities, he was able to get me off the hook. The whole story was kept out of the papers and I was so grateful that I quit using drugs. For about six months, that is. And I continued to drink. By this time most of my behavior had become reduced to seeking the next high. I got off, didn't I? I just had to be more clever next time, that's all.

Delinquency or Disease?

If you're reading this book from an institution such as a jail, detention home, or workhouse and do not yet identify with us, *carefully* and *honestly* evaluate how you got there. Delinquency or disease? Recover or recaught? Which is it? For those of you already convinced you share our problem, don't let resentment of the establishment prevent you from starting on the path of recovery. Just maybe your HP has something in mind for you.

We know there is such a plan. Do first things first, contact outside members of the fellowship, begin working the Steps, and your purpose will become clear. Don't let the vastness of projected outcomes for your future overwhelm you and crumble your foundation. Realize that your Higher Power is ever mindful of you.

Dark Angels

Paranoia strikes often when one is loaded and it even continues to haunt a person in the early stages of sobriety. You may be convinced that the police are making a special effort to trail you, using every law to try and get you. The school system may seem to be constantly hassling you; you may think that your employer will fire you with the least flimsy excuse; your family may call you the black sheep. If you think they're all out to get you, *you may be right.* Look at it this way: you're no angel, even if Mom once thought you were. Upon honest evaluation of our behavior, what do we expect? We've become dark angels to anyone involved in our lives. Didn't we put ourselves in a position for this to happen because of drunk driving, theft, carrying weapons, violence, a flagrant disregard for the happiness or well-being of others, criminal activity, and flipping serious attitude into people's faces?

If we want to stay clean and sober, we *must* change our hostile attitudes toward the police or anyone who appears to hold authority over us. These negative emotions can do nothing but harm us, and flipping "attitude" will only perpetuate already strained relationships. We no longer need to impress friends, be "cool," or prove ourselves to anyone. Phil recalls:

> I used to love to hassle cops. I was always quite pleased when one was killed. I felt like it was a point for our side. I never got hassled bad by cops but thought it cool to hate them and anybody else in uniform. They were hypocrites and looked down on me. Truthfully, I thought everyone looked down on me. Still, it was cool to hate cops.

Often we had developed a closed-minded contempt for teachers, cops, counselors, and other authority figures just on G.P., or general principal. They've been accused by us of narrow-mindedness, living back in the Stone Age,* looking down on us, being hypocrites, pigs, and many more gross and degrading things we won't mention here. Now who is narrow-minded? Who is judging whom? Just because you're young doesn't automatically place others in the Stone Age.

You Don't Know What You Don't Know

In reality, our closed-mindedness has trapped us in what little we know. We think we know it all or at least *all we need to know.* It seldom

---

* We find that as we get older, this is called "experience."

occurs to us, however, that we're unable to learn anything new if we already know it. We don't listen to information when we think we know. If you already know it all, you're basically unteachable. So we ask you to remain open-minded to the suggestions of others, even if they do come from "the establishment." Older people may be able to teach you something; they may not. But in any case, with an open mind, you won't miss valuable opportunities to keep moving forward. Cindy shares how she cultivated an open mind:

> I used to judge all teachers [and adults] as the establishment with which I would have nothing to do. Once I had opened my mind a bit, I found a middle-aged woman whom I could relate to and we became close friends. I opened my mind a little bit more, and I found a teacher who was human and who cared. I am now good friends with that teacher. I found most people are similar to me in many ways. Through opening my eyes, I have found some close friends, and, even more important, I have seen that nothing can be more rewarding than an open mind.

Give Time Time

Maybe you're not in prison but somewhere you don't want to be. For instance, a number of young alcoholics and addicts have been ostracized by their families and end up in group or foster homes. Some families, angry and ashamed, not knowing how to handle these kids, have signed their lives away. Such a situation seems sad and unfortunate to us but occurs more often than we'd like. Give time time. Anything can happen in God's world. Whatever your circumstances, try not to harbor resentments. Resentments, we find, are analogous to drinking poison and expecting the other person to die. Remember, you are part of a larger family now. We're a family who will never turn our backs on you, a family with members who *care*. We really do!

RONDELL'S STORY
She had to get locked up to find her freedom.

As seems to be the case in far too many black families, my brother and I were raised by our mother, with precious little help from my alcoholic father. I don't remember him coming 'round much except when he felt guilty. Because my mother was in the military, she traveled a lot and we stayed with relatives. So although we were a close-knit family, my childhood consisted of an absent father, an often absent mother, and an obligation to care for my younger brother.

At thirteen, my first introduction to alcohol was with the gin and scotch that Mom kept for entertaining. I would invite the boys in the neighborhood over; we played hooky from school, got drunk, and then tore up the house. Drugs came into the picture around this same time. My stepdad, whom I loved deeply, had stomach problems and took Valium for it. I found a bottle of pills and took some. The feeling of relaxation was *wonderful*. I didn't understand that I was opening the doors to hell.

I excelled at school and the progression of my disease came after graduation and after the birth of my child. Oh, my boyfriend, Kevin, and I smoked a little weed, drank wine coolers, and played at being in love. At graduation, I was seventeen and pregnant, but Kevin and I did not marry. I decided to stay home, living with Mom, so I would have adequate care for me and my child.

Javar came early and with many problems. He had a hole in his heart, his intestines were on the outside of his body, and he needed immediate surgery. But I fell in love with my tiny, vulnerable, innocent son. They had to kick me out of the hospital at night because I was by Javar's side constantly.

God Told Me to Check on You
At home I doted on Javar and often cuddled with him in my bed. Part of his care consisted of a drug called theophyline for his asthma condi-

tion. One night the medicine didn't seem to be working. He was congested and wheezing, so I gave my baby a second dose to ease his discomfort. From my bed, I sleepily lay him in his crib. Uncharacteristic of her, my mother burst through the door and cut the light on. Javar was having a seizure! Later she told me, "God told me to check on you."

We raced to the hospital and the whole family arrived in a heartbeat. At first, a really sweet, plump Caucasian nurse consoled me. Behind her came the doctor who said, "Your son died of an overdose." I fainted. My precious baby was not protected by his mother but *was killed* by her! I *could not/would not* say anything about the second dose and immediately blamed the doctors and hospital. They *knew* the medicine was too strong, I cried. I even did research to back up my case, and my cycle of blaming began.

When Javar died in February, something in me died too. Then fate frowned on me again, because in April, the only father I knew blew his brains out. My stepdad had always been able to care for us and make everything better. He was a strong man. But when Javar died, this was something he couldn't make better. In the family's overwhelming grief, I felt he opted out and now I was responsible for two deaths.

Life no longer held meaning for me. I slept around and began sniffing powder cocaine. Although I attempted college for a while, it wasn't long before it interfered with my highs and I dropped out. Then I got pregnant again and wanted to abort. Mom and the family talked me out of that, but I was already totally indifferent to this child.

When Jessica was born, I refused to attach to her. But she became a great excuse to get money from Mom. "Jessica needs this; Jessica needs that; I have bills to pay." Of course, the money went for cocaine. I also figured out how to swipe credit cards through twice at the gas station where I worked to pocket extra money. Naturally I got caught.

"Okay, Crime Does Pay," I Said

Because I had a clean record and had been an excellent student, they only gave me two days. *Two days!* So I said to myself, "Okay, crime does pay." In addition to the system enabling me, my mom was a big-time codependent. She went into total denial about what was happening and picked up all the pieces. My military mom could fix anything. I moved back home with her for a while but applied for public housing. In public housing the drugs flowed, so when Dove Court accepted me, I was relieved. I could use again.

This was a dangerous place. Shots rang through the dark of night. People lurked behind stairwells doing God-knows-what. I could walk out my front door and see twenty guys beating up one and I just stepped around them. You had to mind your own business in Dove Court.

By this time I could only work at odd jobs. At a bottle-packing company I noticed a popular guy with a great smile. I found out Marty was favored by the drug dealers, so I made it a point to get up under him. Marty liked heroin; I liked cocaine. We scored before work, after work, and on breaks.

I Couldn't See I Wasn't a Victim, but a Volunteer

Pretty soon I noticed that my highs were shorter than Marty's. "Let me try some of that stuff," I said. I *loved* heroin instantly, and that began my final decent into hell. I blamed Marty for my downfall. In fact, my whole personal litany became one of blame and victimhood. I was a victim because my first son died; they *made* me have Jessica; Marty hooked me on heroin; I lost my childhood watching my brother; my biological father wasn't there; and my "dad" killed himself.

Soon the odd jobs didn't support my habit of sniffing heroin, so I began a stealing operation. I stole from Wal-Mart, Kmart, Sears, and Penney's, then returned the merchandise for cash. I got caught but the system would never give me any time.

Do the Crime and Whine, Get Very Little Time

By this time I was doing about fifty dollars of heroin a day, mixing it with crack, and sniffing powder. After about seven or eight petty larcenies and very little time, they combined charges and got me for grand larceny. One judge finally gave me ninety days, but I asked for weekends "because of Jessica." The judge let me!

Pregnant again with Marty's child, I showed up for a weekend with heroin, doxepin, Valium, and Clonidine up my vagina. In the shower I took some pills and sniffed heroin and passed out. "Where am I? Where is my dope?" I asked coming to in the hospital.

"Did you know you are pregnant?" the doctor inquired. "What the hell does that have to do with anything?" I asked. I had OD'd and not died. That was the first of many overdoses. Hey, I was invincible. The courts only slapped my hands, my mom always picked up the pieces, and I could live through an overdose. So I got worse. Thank God for the baby; when I went in for my next weekend, they kept me. For most of that pregnancy, I couldn't use. Jahnay was born just a few weeks after my release and then my mom had both my kids.

It wasn't long before I was 117 pounds. At 5'9" that isn't pretty. I couldn't steal 'cause the clerks saw me coming, knew I didn't have money, and shouldn't be there. I prostituted myself, sleeping with men I wouldn't have looked at earlier. I lost all my boundaries, wandering around the streets, disheveled, and washing only when I could find a shower in a crack house or shooting gallery. I was for sale to anybody for anything. My last crime was forgery and uttering when some guy got me to play along with his check scam.

This Time I Got Time

This time I got time and it probably saved my life. They sent me to Pocahontas Correctional Unit, a therapeutic community (TC). I didn't want any part of it. I just wanted to do my time and leave. I shivered beside the cold, thick walls and shrank from the "clunk" when the doors locked. "Okay, I gotta be here so I'll play the game," I whispered.

The cold, thick walls were not unlike the walls I had built since Javar's death. They put me in an expression group where you were expected to work the Steps, get gut level, and put it all out on the floor. Being in this atmosphere and listening to the cons tell their stories, my walls began to crumble. At first I only listened, but eventually realized exactly where my life was at.

Once I accepted God into my life, I became willing and open to do *anything* to turn my life around. I desperately wanted change and needed direction, and whatever they said would help is what I clung to. I didn't care if it was twenty Steps; *I'd do it.*

I Could See the Culprit and She Was Me

What I like about the Twelve Steps is how they work together as a process; one Step takes you to the next and the next—*it's a life.* So the Twelve Steps began their process with me, not me with them.

My favorite Step is One, where I admitted my problem. It went along with the phases in the TC. After orientation, I got phased up where you become accountable. I got wrote up and confronted a few times and began to realize I couldn't get away with everything. There were no lenient judges or a codependent mother to let me get away with things. I realized I wasn't a victim any longer who could blame everyone and everything else—I could see the culprit and she was me!

I got fearful the closer it came to my release date, and I experienced withdrawal again—the sweats and cramps. After two years of clean time, I was terrified. "I need more help," I begged, and so they set me up at Serenity House for transitional living. I've been here a week now. Although I have two years' clean time, I only claim this week when out. Sure I'm restricted here, but an addict doesn't know restrictions. This is show-and-tell time!

My children came up to see me yesterday with my mom. God has rebuilt that bridge with my kids. *I love my kids.* I'll probably never understand God's ways, why Javar was taken so early. But I'm grateful that God protected my little angels, Jessica and Jahnay, from my addiction, both in the womb and out.

For those of you considering recovery, you don't have to go as low as I did. You don't have to go to the penitentiary to realize that you're the cause of your own problems. Take it from me; it's not "them!" It was getting locked up that set me free. What's it going to take to set you free?

CHAPTER 9
Yes, But . . .

"I doubted the program would work for me (after all, I was different!)."
—Kathy

Whether or not you think you're in the same class as the people in this book is something only you can decide. If you believe there's still a good time waiting for you in a bottle, a fix, a tab, or a bag—nothing in *Young, Sober & Free* is going to stop you. We're hoping that you'll learn from our experience. Some of us are able to learn from others' mistakes and the rest of us have to make the mistakes! We hope you are the former.

There Is No Right Way to Do the Wrong Thing

One thing we're all clever at is excuses that seemingly make our self-centered behavior look reasonable. Having lied to ourselves and others for a long time makes it difficult now to recognize the truth. When you say, "Well, I identify with a lot of what you're saying and I think I might be chemically dependent, but I haven't had the D.T.'s, OD'd, been in jail, lost a wife, been shot, or tested positive for HIV," just attach *yet* to it. We hope your brain isn't so fried that you fail to realize the progressive nature of addiction and how it persistently pushes you into doing things that are degrading, humiliating, violent, self-centered, and sad. Amanda is only sixteen years old, yet the disease is very aggressive in her—in a few short months this is how fast her addiction progressed:

> I'd break into my dad's house and take anything that was there. Then one day at the mall I met this guy and we got stoned.

115

That night I did mushrooms, Ecstasy, crank; smoked weed; and drank until seven in the morning. For the next three days we got sooo coked up and I pleaded for him to take me to my hometown. He finally agreed and I met up with my friend "Ann." I ended up living with this guy Joe for about six months. We did coke all day and all night. Then "Ann" and I went and found an abandoned house and we decided to live in it. This was around the first time I did heroin. I don't remember much but lying on the ground trying to keep my head up. Around then, my very best friend, who was also my aunt, was murdered. I decided to move in with my mom again but screwed up so bad I got kicked out. For the next five months I stole about two thousand dollars and stole dope too. I kept on the move and finally had a mental breakdown and cut myself and wound up in a psychiatric ward.

Our disease usually doesn't let up until we're locked up, locked down, or dead. You don't have to get as bad as Amanda did, but then again, maybe you do.

Facing the Light or Feeling the Heat?

This book shares our model of sobriety in the hope that you'll face the light, thus allowing the shadows to fall behind. Some of us change when we see the light. Most of us change when we feel the heat! We'd like to be totally optimistic in our approach and say, "You have it made! You're out of the darkness forever." Unfortunately, we know that more of us die from the disease than ever recover from it. But reading this far shows an amount of willingness on your part. We can truthfully say that for the willing, the chances of recovery are excellent, providing you avoid the traps that have ensnared far too many of us. For simplicity's sake, we've labeled these the "Yes, but . . ." traps and hope that you review them without saying "Yes, but . . ."

Trap Number One: Yes, but there are times I have to take drugs.

In AA we've been told that alcohol is "cunning, baffling, and power-ful" and for us that applies to all mind-affecting chemicals. Our disease beckons us in many subtle ways. For instance, we get headaches, tooth-aches, allergies, and coughs; find we can't sleep at night; or develop the "crazies" and all kinds of psychosomatic and/or real physical compli-cations with which we con ourselves and our physicians into believing we need pills. This is a deadly con game. Suzi had this experience:

> About six months after becoming sober I began having head-aches, went to a doctor, and was prescribed Librium. I got loaded and was off and running again. Everything I'd gained through sobriety was gone. I again experienced compulsion. I knew I was going down and couldn't stop. Through the grace of God and the help of people in the program, I was able to start with my new way of life again. I returned to the only honest position: I accepted that I was totally chemically ad-dicted. Today I believe that if I can say, "Yes, I need something for my pain," then I probably don't need anything at all. It's surprising how much pain we can take when we turn to God instead of pills.

This isn't to say that one takes nothing if severely injured or in a life-threatening situation. Our purpose is to live; the reason we abstain is to stay alive. The value isn't *not to use;* the value is *life.* So if, under life-threatening circumstances, a doctor determines that we *need* medi-cation to live, then life takes the priority. We ask for the protection of our Higher Power and accept the situation. Fortunately, it's only *very* rarely that any of us would be in such a situation.

Do Not Let Others Practice Medicine on You
At other times, however, we must regularly take certain medicines that some people in the fellowships deem "mind-affecting." These medicines fall into the classes of drugs that treat the brain chemistry imbalances in depression, schizophrenia, phobias, and other similar disturbances. Some functional diseases like epilepsy and fibromyalgia also call for

medicines some clean and sober people consider questionable. These are the psychoactive drugs that alter a user's moods, perceptions, feelings, personality, or behavior and can potentially be abused.

Medicines are used to treat and prevent illness and *some medicines are psychoactive.* If you're diagnosed with any of the disorders that call for psychoactive drugs, you and your physician must decide what medicines are appropriate for you. Your doctor should be well versed in chemical dependency and completely familiar with your addiction. Don't let your friends, sponsor, or other program members practice medicine on you. On the other hand, don't let your addictive voice exaggerate symptoms just so your inner addict can get drugs. Taking medicines is a delicate balancing act; you and your physician must address this issue up front, and then you must monitor the situation with impeccable honesty.

Sometimes Take an Aspirin and Adjust!

Realize, though, that rationalization can lurk behind every thought. That's why we put the word *impeccable* before honesty. Our disease influences our mind in exhausting and varied ways (the addictive voice within ever lurking), causing us to justify taking mind-affecting chemicals. Consider this: you have a broken toe and say, "I can't live with this pain." *Nonsense.* Of course you can; take an aspirin and adjust! You'll surprise yourself at just how much you can do without the aid of chemicals. In fact, as soon as your head *knows* you're not going to take pills, the pain will lessen immediately. The suggestion most of us follow is this: get a doctor who *knows addiction* and follow his or her advice. Don't self-prescribe.

Trap Number Two: Yes, but what will I tell my friends?

You'll make many new friends in recovery. We guarantee that your new life will include a whole new set of friends. If your old friends didn't do drugs with you, you have nothing to worry about anyway. But we suspect that you hung out with the kids doing what you wanted to do—drugs. Gary shares how his decision to stay clean and sober affected him:

> I had a lot of fear when I quit getting loaded because that's all I ever did with my friends. I was afraid they'd think I was a turkey. So I had to decide which was more important: my life and sanity or what people thought of me. If they were true friends, they'd want only the best for me. I soon found I had very few friends from my past.

Once you choose to unconditionally accept this new life, you probably won't want to hang out or hook up with anyone from the using crowd. But that doesn't mean life will be dull. Kim expressed it this way:

> It's true that because my sobriety comes first now, I have to give up some people I've known as friends. At one time, these people meant more to me than I meant to myself. They love drugs more than they love me—or themselves. I don't blame them; I still love them, but I have to live with myself, not with them. I need my ability to think and I cherish my sanity. I give them the freedom to be who they are, as they must allow me the same. Who knows? Maybe one day they'll find the freedom I've found.

Trap Number Three: Yes, but what about peer pressure?

Peer pressure? This is a cop-out too. We find it isn't so much *pressure* but *preference*. When you're with your buddies, you want to be like them. Of course. Who wants to be the odd man out? So we stop the rhetoric about peer pressure and call it what it is, *peer preference*. This is more honest. So if you find yourself hanging out at raves, sitting in cars with friends smoking weed, or in a neighborhood gang meeting, you're in the wrong place because you've made a choice, not because of any pressure.

If You're in the Wrong Place, the Right Place Is Empty

We must admit that there's only one real reason we would hang out with our using friends and that's because, deep down, we still want to use. Sooner or later we'll be "pressured" into it, when actually it was our preference—*our choice* in the first place. Remember, too, that if you're in the wrong place, the right place is empty.

Once you decide where the right place and wrong place is, what about these "peers" of yours? In the Twelve Step fellowships you'll find yourself at a whole new level with your peers. Your peers today are people in recovery, not some same-age group. Your peers may be fifteen or fifty; age is not what makes us peers. It's our desire to recover and to carry the message of recovery to others that binds us to each other. So stop thinking of yourself and your peers as anyone of a certain age, culture, or look. Look to your *real* peers: a new family in the fellowship of the spirit.

Some folks in the fellowships may try to put you in a different "younger" class. Don't let them do it. We're all only one drink away from a drunk, one hit away from a high.

Trap Number Four: Yes, but why me?

This is an interesting snare, catching people who go out and get loaded because they resent having this disease. The "Why me?" is akin to the "Poor me." And we know about the "Poor me" trap: *Poor me; poor me; pour me a drink.*

Whiners Don't Win and Winners Don't Whine

Asking "Why me?" is similar to asking oneself, "Why do I have red hair; why am I left-handed, double jointed, born in Kansas, one sex or the other?" or the classic, "Why am I alive?" These questions are basically unanswerable, or, at the most, the answers are extremely subjective. Our suggestion: Be a winner, not a whiner.

Trap Number Five: Yes, but I'll never have any fun anymore.

Believe us, living life to its fullest is much more fun and exciting than any fogged-up, drug-distorted life we led in the past. Our gatherings are marked by laughter, love, sharing, and caring.

Do you think you could be bored with the spare time you might have? Let us assure you, *there won't be* any spare time. In between school, work, and meetings, you'll be taking your Steps, talking to your sponsor, and Twelfth Stepping. Then there are conventions, regionals, round-ups, parties, and other clean and sober group activities to choose from. You also have a responsibility to your home group: business meetings, cleanup, refreshments, and possibly service work. With your new interest in life, you undoubtedly will start new projects or hobbies. You may even find yourself in church on Sunday morning. Frankly, if you're anything like us, you'll be lucky to squeeze in three decent meals and eight hours sleep in any given day. Jimmie P. says:

> In my first six months of sobriety I went to more of the places I had talked of going to but had never gotten around to. I met more people than I had met in the last two years of using. I did more exciting things than I had ever imagined possible with my old way of thinking. And, amazingly, I remember them all!

Trap Number Six: Yes, but I'll never be as perfect as the rest of you seem to be.

Hold on a moment! Perfection is not our goal, or our status. We claim progress, not perfection. Oh, we have our fair share of problems; we just work on them all the time. Shelly put it this way:

> I was constantly beating myself over the head when I was drinking for not living up to my morals and values. I thought this would stop once I worked the Steps, but it didn't. In my first year, my sponsor asked me what I was doing. Well, I was running the young people's Tuesday night meeting, working a

Fourth and Fifth Step, trying to quit smoking, eating health food to clear out my body, serving as a representative from my home group to the larger governing body of the program, praying for patience—about this time, she stopped me. Elaine told me my goals were close to perfect and I was far from perfect. So, of course, I couldn't live up to them. I had to set them where they were in my reach. "Progress, not perfection," she chided.

Trap Number Seven: Yes, but they're all old fogies at the meetings; I can't relate.

We know it can seem strange to sit in a roomful of older folks talking about their drinking and drugging days. Some of them might still call marijuana "grass" or refer to "goof balls," "skank," or "horse" as their drugs of choice. "What outdated slang and lame lives they lead" are some of the things you may tell yourself. "I'm different; I don't relate; there's a generation gap."

You *Are* Unique, Just Like the Rest of Us
Something about addicts often gets in our way. It's this feeling that we're

- unique
- different
- better than
- worse than
- older
- younger
- hipper
- smarter

We think we're just unique enough that this program won't work for us. This is a function of the addictive voice within. Most members come to their first few meetings finding every reason in the world why they're not like "those" people. When we're young, it's easy to focus on the most glaring "difference"—age—when our addictive voice talks to us. This is simply our disease struggling for survival, trying to convince us that we're different and don't belong. After all, if we belong, then we might get well and how will the addict within survive?

To combat this excuse, members in the meetings have learned to tell newcomers concerned about "religion," "If the God-talk runs you out, the booze will run you back," or if potential members are concerned about being with the lower classes, they're told, "If the cussing drives you out, the drugs will drive you back." And so on. In our case, we can say something to young newcomers along the lines of, "If the wisdom in the rooms runs you out, the wreckage in your life will run you back," or "If the experience at these tables blows you away, E-bombs will blow you back!"

Then there's the infuriating habit of older folks patronizing us. It does happen on occasion. It drives Bethany wild when people say, "You're so lucky to be here at such a young age." Or with Lori:

> I still get the "You're too young to be an alcoholic" or the "I spilled more than you drank." But those remarks don't bother me because now I have the rest of my life to live.

These types of remarks are not about you; *they're about them.* They are the regrets from their own lost and wasted years. Lori went on to say:

> Today I also realize that age has nothing to do with this disease and that it truly is a disease. No matter what our age, we all share the same feelings.

Trap Number Eight: Yes, but I had a problem with crack cocaine, not alcohol, so I can surely have a beer now and then.

If you're still telling yourself this and pretending you still don't "get it" (that addiction is addiction is addiction), then you're probably not finished using yet. We understand some well-meaning adults not "getting it." It isn't their disease. Unless they went through addiction education with you, they're likely to be really ignorant on this issue. For you, though, this is no excuse, even if an adult goes along with the plan. T. J. had this to say about his experience once he got out of treatment and into a sober high school:

It's hard to try and stay sober when you don't want it. I made it a month sober once I got out of rehab into a sober high school. Then one of my friends from rehab had a dad who let him drink a little. So I hung with him and we drank on weekends. I lied to everyone about my drinking, then drank to forget I lied.

T. J. let the ignorance of his friend's dad allow him to practice his disease. But we know our disease and know that a drug is a drug is a drug. For Phil it was different. His dad was in AA and so Phil knew that alcohol was liquid drugs, but he rationalized anyway:

Testing [controlled drinking] was just an excuse to get high once more. Four days later I was loaded before I went to work, and I had said I would never do that. Fear of dying came over me so intensely, I can't describe it. I could see I was killing myself. I hated my guts so much I couldn't stand to look in the mirror. I knew in my heart that I was powerless over weed and other drugs, but I felt I could handle booze. I stayed in the same pattern I had been in since I was twelve. I soon found I was drinking more than I had been, feeling the same feelings of guilt and fear, and hiding the fact that I was drinking from the people closest to me.

Although people say "experience is the best teacher," in our case mistakes can be fatal. Learn from our experience, *please*. This isn't the time to be fooling around, especially when living and dying are the alternatives.

Reality Has a Way of Screwing Up Our Fantasies

If you haven't already made it, you're on the brink of making the single greatest decision of your life. This requires you to take a good long look at yourself, your life, and where your decisions have led you to now.

Reality check.
You are here:

Now honestly tell yourself where "here" is for you. Have your decisions put you in the place you want to be? Here's what Phil saw at this point in his recovery:

> The life I was trapped in before AA had a very definite direction and destination. As I looked down the road of that life, it contained many things: wrecked cars, hospitals, broken friendships, broken homes, hate, fear, despair, on and on. But worst of all, I had to walk down that road with a person I despised—myself!

Since Phil made his decision, this is how he sees life:

> The road I'm on now has a direction, but I see no end. The only limits I see are the limits I put on it. In God's eyes, it's limitless. It's a joy to be filled with the prospect of learning to live in love, to accept my humanness, and not to feel defeated because of it. The Twelve Steps of AA are tools. They can keep us dry and clean if that's all we want, but sobriety is a neverending process. If we decide we want more, we can have more at any time. The Twelve Steps, worked honestly, will keep us on that road—growing and growing and growing.

Working the Twelve Steps doesn't eliminate skepticism and doubt.

We'll try to talk ourselves out of this new way of life at various vulnerable times and so will others. Joey remembers:

> Once I was at the park and saw this guy I used to see at meetings but hadn't been around for a while. He pulled out a Bible and told me that AA wasn't for him. He said, "If you talk about the past, it's a sin." I really started questioning my program. But one of my friends told me that fanatics will say all kinds of things like, "You're not powerless over some bit of alcoholic liquid, are you?" So I relaxed, realizing I don't have to get worked up just because some fanatic talks trash.

Whatever arises, we know that "This, too, shall pass." What really grabs our attention and strengthens our faith are the thousands of recovering young people today. The glow on their faces, the repaired lives, the united families, and the laughter that echoes from church basements, private homes, sober high schools, and Alano clubs. We've discovered the secret to living a happy, full life. Not problem-free, perhaps, but what were once stumbling blocks are now stepping-stones.

YES, Youth Enjoying Sobriety

The shortest sentence in the Big Book, the granddaddy of all our Twelve Step programs, is, "It works." The brevity and simplicity of this message cannot be said any better when referring to our Twelve Step recovery. In closing, we can think of nothing more profound. We are *Youth Enjoy Sobriety*, the YES crowd in the fellowship. Hopefully, and with the grace of God, we will cross paths on our clean and sober journey. In the meantime, our final message for you is, forget the "Yes, buts . . ." and remember:

"*Yes*, it works."

ANDY'S STORY

*"At seventeen, I look back at where I came from and where I am now
and I can't believe the difference. It's great not to have to remember
all the lies I told to cover my tracks."*

My story isn't different from anyone else's. We alcoholics and addicts
are all the same. Oh, maybe our financial situation, our childhood play-
grounds, our religion and race are different, *but our stories are basically
the same:* we drank alcohol and used drugs; at first they seemed to solve
our problems; eventually they created more problems than they solved;
finally, we had to have help to stop the destructive cycle of addiction.
So here's our story.

I grew up in a white middle-class home with two loving parents
and two loving sisters. Right from the beginning I showed a lot of the
signs of being an alcoholic. Lying, stealing, and cheating meant nothing to me if it led to me getting my way. As amazing as it is, even as a
little kid, I felt left out of life, alone, and different. There was this
emptiness inside that demanded to be filled and my childhood memo-
ries are riddled with this relentless need to fill this gapping hole.

Inside, I Was a Scared, Unsure Little Kid

The solution presented itself when my parents gave me my first beer. I
was ten. It was their goal to teach me how to drink responsibly at an
early age. That night I found the missing piece to life. *It was alcohol.*
From that day on I knew what I needed to succeed in life and my parents supplied it at dinner. At ten, I only drank with my parents, but
two years later I began hanging out with my older sister's boyfriends.
They drank and it fit my style. I did whatever they did because I wanted
to fit in.

Drinking was wonderful because it erased any guilt I felt as the
me-me-me boy, created by lying, cheating, and stealing to get what I

wanted. These older people accepted me for me, or at least that's what I thought. It was all a facade. Oh, how I wanted to be a big badass but knew inside that I was a scared, unsure little kid. I drank whenever I could so that the badass in me would scare the little kid away.

Entering junior high made me feel I was alone in the world. All these other kids were so immature and I was a badass. The badass just didn't fit in with these people. The few friends I did collect weren't genuine. I was a doormat whom everyone at school walked over. All that just made me want to drink even more. By thirteen my tolerance had already increased and it took too much beer to get loaded, so I had to switch to hard liquor.

For Forty-five Bucks I Attended a Twenty-Hour Party

My friends were twenty-two and twenty-three. I did things with them that fit my picture of myself and built my ego. We hung out and went to raves like the USC2 in Seattle. At this yearly event, they never checked your age and for forty-five bucks I attended a twenty-hour party. Raves were fun and the people liked me and they didn't walk all over me. Besides I've always liked techno, could take Ecstasy, and drink all I wanted.

EGO: Edging God Out

At the age of fifteen, I started living a double life. In one life I was nice, caring, and proper, and in the alternate I was a mean, knife-wielding thief. I liked my drinking self best. He was a big shot who could handle his liquor. This big shot was the person I wanted to be. Any possible bridges of friendship with the kids at school were burned by the big shot because he created so much conflict. So I found people who liked to be with people like me—drinkers with egos like mine. These new friends encouraged my drinking and let me run with it. My ego just shot off like a missile and I was the king of the universe. One night out drinking with these new friends, I ended up stealing a car and then blowing it up for fun. I didn't really know why I did it. My conscience kicked in and told me it was wrong. As usual, I drank more allowing the big shot to chase that scared little kid with a conscience away.

In the summer just before high school, I found that I couldn't deal with life on life's terms. I told myself that life had treated me badly and it wasn't my fault. I decided that accepting God into my life would fix all my problems. I kept on drinking while going to church thinking I was so holy. But why didn't life get better? In the fall of that year, I gave up the whole God thing because one problem after another kept dogging me.

Sobriety Is Not a Dress Rehearsal

Some *real* friends that I had from my neighborhood decided to blackmail me. They threatened to tell my folks about my drinking if I didn't go to AA. I went, but my mind kept telling me, "How can I be an alcoholic when I'm an honor student and I haven't ever been in trouble for drinking?" I hung around the fellowship for about three months until one night, I got a case of the "Yes, buts . . ." and I went out to find this bottom they spoke of.

I got my first job at a local country club working as a busboy. All I had to do was pick up dirty plates. Not long after starting there, I found the liquor room and snuck a copy of the key. Here sat an endless supply of whatever I wanted. I found I was doing a daily program just like they said in AA, only it was a daily program of drinking. Again, I found older people who liked my style and everyone but my parents knew. Eventually I got careless. My dad caught me with a case of beer, weed, and Ecstasy in the trunk when I was leaving to party with my friends. Mom started calling parents and they grounded me. "You can golf and go to work," they said to punish me. Great, I thought. I drank when I golfed and I drank when I worked. This was sweet.

Homeboys Shopping Network

At the beginning of my junior year in high school, my need for alcohol was overwhelming. I took to carrying a water bottle of vodka. I perched it boldly right on my desk. My girlfriend got fed up and told me to stop drinking, so I started to do Ecstasy because it was the craze. But my friend, the bottle, was my priority and in a couple weeks I was nursing that again. I lied, cheated, and stole from everyone to support my lifestyle. My friends and I began the "Homeboys Shopping Network" located in the trunk of my car. You placed an order, and we went and got it. I stole alcohol, a car, golf clubs, money, CDs, car speakers and stereos—whatever anyone wanted.

The perfect life I created didn't last long. I got caught at school with my "water" bottle—they told me to see a drug counselor. My boss at work noticed I was out of it and I unabashedly admitted to drinking Jack Daniels. At home my dad found a stash of bottles in my car. All this came down in the same week!

They sent me to an inpatient treatment center, and I was kicked out after the first day. "I don't need your help," I told them. "You're out," they replied, because it was only a center for those who wanted help. So my folks sent me to a lockdown with cameras to watch me and bolts on the doors to keep me in. Since I had nothing better to do, I began to listen. Maybe these people did know something I didn't.

It was the hardest thing that I had to do, admitting that I was at the base of all my problems. It made perfect sense that the problem wasn't alcohol; *it was all about me.* During my time in there, I realized that I had a problem—not many people drink two to three fifths of vodka a week. Once I admitted the problem was me, the rest came easier. I started seeing through the lies that I'd told everyone, most of all myself. They kept me in there for forty-five days.

Seven Days without a Meeting Makes One Weak

Post-treatment, I joined AA, not to keep my parents from finding out who I really was, but for me to find out who I really was. I did what was recommended in the fellowship, got a sponsor, and went to meetings almost daily. I heard, "Seven days without a meeting makes one weak," and I took it to heart. As time passed I began to understand what this program is all about; it's a daily thing not a onetime fix-it. This means that practicing principles and attending meetings are important. I now find that I can look at myself and know who I am. I don't have to please anyone else. Selfish? Yes. They say this is a selfish program but we can't be self-centered. What we do is make our own spiritual program our priority, which is selfish; that enables us to work with others, which is not selfish and self-centered; that in turn keeps us sober, which is selfish again! We're all selfish; I'm no different from anyone else. Well, yes, I am. I'm unique, just like everyone else!

I've found a whole new life in the halls of AA. Some people say I'm too young to have a problem, but that doesn't bother me. This isn't about them; it's about me and I know my addiction and my recovery. That's all that matters. As I grow spiritually, I find myself becoming increasingly honest with myself and others. I still do some of the foolish things that I did in the past. Hey, I'm young. The only difference is that I know when I'm wrong and don't run. That scared little kid inside has matured and now faces the "badass" head-on when he tries to take over.

At seventeen, I look back at where I came from and where I am now and I can't believe the difference. It's great not to have to remember all the lies I told to cover my tracks. I don't have to be with people I don't like just to drink with them. Now I've found real friends who care about me and don't care about my past. They just care about me. And they trust me. So do my parents! In fact, people listen to me today because they know I live by principles and seek to be honest. They know they can ask me something and that I won't lie. Adults seldom trust teens, but they trust me.

So this is my story, this is our story, and with a little bit of effort on your part, it can be your story too.

NOEL'S STORY
Desperately, she sought to fill the emptiness in herself.

I had one of these normal childhoods. You know the kind—full of lone-liness, insecurity, remorse, fear, low self-esteem, and dishonesty. But I didn't have all those fancy words for it before. All I remember was that it felt *bad*. No, I wasn't an orphan or a product of a broken home. Actu-ally I don't know what made me a drunk, but it happened.

My dad was in the service and our family moved around a lot. There was fear in my childhood about making new friends. "What do I say?" "How do I act?" I remember the constant feeling of *not knowing*. I didn't know the people around me, I didn't know what to do so they'd like me, and I didn't know what was wrong with me. I always had the feeling that I wasn't as good as they were. I would see people around me and they were so smart. All the girls who wore pretty flowered dresses made me jealous. Those girls seemed to be able to talk to the boys and I couldn't. Everyone around seemed to have friends but me.

The Other Kids Were Playing Kissy-Kissy
Near the end of the fourth grade, the most popular boy in the class had a party, and everyone was invited. Even me. I recall sitting on the porch and slowly, slowly all the kids went around to the side of the house. One other girl and I were left. The vague idea that the other kids were playing kissy-kissy was in my head. Then two boys walked up to us. One boy said to the other, "She's cute; let's get her." And they took the other girl off to the side too. And I sat munching on a cupcake; I re-member that it didn't feel too good on the inside. I began to hate those people then, but I still wanted them to like me.

At our family get-togethers there would usually be lots of liquor. I would always sneak a little. Somehow I knew that the secret to being happy was hidden inside that bottle. Later, I would tell my friends about how much I drank; a little lying would make me okay. I just wanted to be loved. This search for approval didn't always lead me astray; in one way, it helped.

Getting High without Drugs

Where I lived, there was a group of people, Palmer Drug Abuse Program, much like AA except that most of the people were from ages thirteen to twenty-five. Here was a group of people who seemed to be happy and didn't even get high. I couldn't believe it. They had a loving, fantastic fellowship and I wanted to be a part of it. They said it was simple: just make meetings, stay sober, and follow these Twelve Steps.

However, the part about the Twelve Steps was something else. Hell, I didn't really have a problem; why should I follow these Steps? They said the answers to all my troubles were there, that's why. So for the next six months I stuck with this program, stayed sober, and followed the Third Step—a little. Most of the Steps I followed by picking and choosing. I eliminated Step One, the Fifth Step inventory, and whatever else seemed uncomfortable.

I Found a Hole Inside and Just Kept Digging

With this attitude I made little progress. And I still had this big hole inside me that needed to be filled. After all that time of sticking around and staying straight, I still wanted to get high. "I could," I conned myself. "I was in control." Little by little, I stopped hanging around people in the program and started to run around with people who got high. And sure enough, it was only a matter of time till I got high.

The details of the next half-year are not important. All that's important is that I spent a lot of time and energy trying to fill the hole inside that refused to be filled. I was sure that the secret still was inside that bottle, but I could never find it. Bottle after bottle was poured into that hole deep inside me, never filling it, never patching me up.

Misery surrounded me. I couldn't understand why nothing worked.

Finally, when I had about a half a day's dryness, I went to a meeting, a special twenty-four-hour-long meeting. Everyone around me laughed and had fun. They felt loved and serene and I felt one inch tall. I sat through that entire meeting feeling *bad*. The hole inside was still there.

Sick and Tired of Being Sick and Tired

A couple of days later something happened. I got sick and tired of being sick and tired. I didn't want that feeling anymore. The people with the faded blue jeans and the empty look had nothing more to offer me. I had to make a decision, and it was that the program and sobriety were the only way. For the first time in my life I was willing to do anything to stay sober, and I knew I couldn't do it by myself. I had to have a Higher Power.

With my back up against a wall, I gave up. Finally I said it and meant it: "I can't, He can, I think I'll let Him." The fight was over, the struggle gone, and that felt *good*. The result was that I stopped digging where the hole was. Where booze had poured right through that emptiness, love, sharing, and caring started to stick around the edges. The more I got, the more that stuck, until finally the hole was filled.

For the next two and one-half years, good replaced bad, openness replaced mad, happy replaced sad. The Twelve Steps have been my path to completeness. There still are hard times because growing is usually painful, but I'm neither alone nor empty. We do this together. *All* our Steps say *We,* not *I.*

The things I have learned are indescribable, but let me mention a few:

- Today I can love myself *and* others.
- I deserve to stay clean and sober.
- I know everything is going to be okay. I've gained serenity.
- God is in control. I don't have to carry that burden any longer.
- I can give what I have been given so freely—experience, strength, and hope.

• When I think things cannot get any better, they often do.
• People love me. I am not alone.

These things are available to all of us. I know that my completeness can be your completeness too. We are here, hoping for you, praying that you find some of what we have, and we'll help you patch your soul, repairing all the holes in your life.

The Twelve Steps of Alcoholics Anonymous

1. We admitted we were powerless over alcohol—that our lives had become unmanageable.
2. Came to believe that a Power greater than ourselves could restore us to sanity.
3. Made a decision to turn our will and our lives over to the care of God *as we understood Him.*
4. Made a searching and fearless moral inventory of ourselves.
5. Admitted to God, to ourselves, and to another human being the exact nature of our wrongs.
6. Were entirely ready to have God remove all these defects of character.
7. Humbly asked Him to remove our shortcomings.
8. Made a list of all persons we had harmed, and became willing to make amends to them all.
9. Made direct amends to such people wherever possible, except when to do so would injure them or others.
10. Continued to take personal inventory and when we were wrong promptly admitted it.
11. Sought through prayer and meditation to improve our conscious contact with God *as we understood Him,* praying only for knowledge of His will for us and the power to carry that out.
12. Having had a spiritual awakening as the result of these steps, we tried to carry this message to alcoholics, and to practice these principles in all our affairs.

The Twelve Steps of AA are taken from *Alcoholics Anonymous,* 4th ed., published by AA World Services, Inc., New York, N.Y., 59–60. Reprinted with permission of AA World Services, Inc. (See editor's note on copyright page.)

The Twelve Steps of Chemically Dependent Anonymous

1. We admitted we were powerless over mood-changing and mind-altering chemicals and that our lives had become unmanageable.
2. We came to believe that a Power greater than ourselves could restore us to sanity.
3. We made a decision to turn our wills and our lives over to the care of God *as we understood Him.*
4. We made a searching and fearless moral inventory of ourselves.
5. We admitted to God, to ourselves, and to another human being the exact nature of our wrongs.
6. We were entirely ready to have God remove all these defects of character.
7. We humbly asked Him to remove our shortcomings.
8. We made a list of all persons we had harmed and became willing to make amends to them all.
9. We made direct amends to such people wherever possible, except when to do so would injure them or others.
10. We continued to take personal inventory and when we were wrong promptly admitted it.
11. We sought through prayer and meditation to improve our conscious contact with God *as we understood Him,* praying only for knowledge of His will for us and the power to carry that out.
12. Having had a spiritual awakening as the result of these steps, we tried to carry this message to other chemically addicted persons and to practice these principles in all our affairs.

Reprinted with permission from CDA Communications, Inc. Adapted from the Twelve Steps of Alcoholics Anonymous with permission of AA World Services, Inc., New York, N.Y. (See editor's note on copyright page.)

The Twelve Steps of Narcotics Anonymous

1. We admitted that we were powerless over our addiction, that our lives had become unmanageable.
2. We came to believe that a Power greater than ourselves could restore us to sanity.
3. We made a decision to turn our will and our lives over to the care of God *as we understood Him.*
4. We made a searching and fearless moral inventory of ourselves.
5. We admitted to God, to ourselves, and to another human being the exact nature of our wrongs.
6. We were entirely ready to have God remove all these defects of character.
7. We humbly asked Him to remove our shortcomings.
8. We made a list of all persons we had harmed, and became willing to make amends to them all.
9. We made direct amends to such people wherever possible, except when to do so would injure them or others.
10. We continued to take personal inventory and when we were wrong promptly admitted it.
11. We sought through prayer and meditation to improve our conscious contact with God *as we understood Him,* praying only for knowledge of His will for us and the power to carry that out.
12. Having had a spiritual awakening as a result of these steps, we tried to carry this message to addicts, and to practice these principles in all our affairs.

Index

About the Author

Since her own recovery at age twenty-one, Shelly Marshall has dedicated her life to working with adolescents and young adults in recovery from alcoholism and other drug addictions. She acquired her training as a Human Service Worker: Specialty Drugs/Alcohol and Certified Substance Abuse Counselor in order to help spread the message of recovery to young people. Little did she know when compiling the first edition of *Young, Sober & Free,* when Shelly *was* a young person in recovery, that she would one day admit her own daughter to a treatment center that would give her daughter this book! Today, beginning with Marshall's mother and extending to her brother, uncles, cousins, and, yes, her daughter, there are more than two hundred years of clean and sober time in her core family. Her goals focus on sharing this hope of recovery with families around the globe.

Marshall specializes in training counselors who work with young addicts, makes presentations internationally, serves as an NGO representative to the United Nations for a Russian Charity NAN (No to Alcoholism and Drug Addiction), and runs several successful Web sites providing information to parents, professionals, and young people regarding addiction and recovery.

Her research has been published in five peer-reviewed, professional/scholarly journals, making Marshall world-recognized as a leader in youth recovery from addiction. From Russia to New Zealand, she gives workshops and does consulting for those who work with youth. Her contributions have been, and continue to be, significant in the addictions field as an author, columnist, international trainer, youth advocate, and researcher into treatment and recovery. This has earned her the respect of her colleagues, which is reflected in the words of Father Joe Martin:

> *She stands as a beacon of simplicity in a world of confusion. I recommend her work highly.*

For more information on young people and recovery, visit Marshall's Web site at www.day-by-day.org.